M

Joe Falls:
50 Years of Sports Writing

(And I still can't tell the difference between a slider and a curve)

by Joe Falls

SPORTS PUBLISHING INC.
A Division of Sagamore Publishing
Champaign, IL 61820

Editor, book layout: Susan M. McKinney
Dustjacket design: Julie L. Denzer
Book and photo insert design: Michelle R. Dressen
Front cover illustration: Dick Mayer

ISBN: 1-57167-176-5
Library of Congress Catalog Card Number: 97-61763

Printed in the United States.

SPORTS PUBLISHING INC.
a division of Sagamore Publishing
804 N. Neil
Champaign, IL 61820

To Ted Smits, who made all this possible.

Contents

Acknowledgments

A special thanks to my agent, Jane Johnson, for her encouragement, patience and professionalism. Also, for her potato salad.

Introduction

Our lives have changed. Television. Drugs. Computers. All in the second half of this century. Sports have changed, too, and I don't mean money, money, money, though this seems like the most important thing of our time.

The games have changed, but so have the athletes and even the fans. Sports have grown so large that (1) it is impossible to keep up with everything anymore and (2) those who try don't seem to have time for any other life.

I am 69 years old and sports editor of *The Detroit News* (really, a columnist) and I come from a time when there were six teams in hockey, 16 in baseball, 12 in football and 12 in basketball. No trouble keeping up at all. Baseball ended the first week of October, football was finished with the bowl games on January 1, hockey ran until the first week of April and basketball to the middle of April. Very orderly. I liked it because the seasons were clearly defined—and I mean winter, spring, summer and autumn.

Now, there are so many games in so many parts of the continent that all the sports lap over into the others and it can get very confusing. They play full schedules—longer than ever—and when it is over, they tell us that that didn't count—here come the playoffs. We fall for it every year.

I used to know every player on the Montreal Canadiens—what they looked like, how they skated, how they shot, how they did everything on the ice. I even knew if they were losing their hair, not that it mattered, except it created an intimacy that added to my pleasure of watching them perform. I knew all these things because I saw the Canadiens seven times a year—more in the playoffs—and this helped in the enjoyment of these games. I could tell whether they were playing well or having an off night, and you could build up some real hatreds against the likes of Dickie (Ding Dong) Moore, Butch Bouchard and even Maurice Richard, who tried to tell us he was better than Gordie Howe. No way, my man. Never in history.

Expansion was inevitable because so much money was there to be made, and television made it all possible. But more hasn't been better. Only more confusing. The Montreal Canadiens now visit Detroit only once a year—they are here and they are gone. I have no idea who plays on the first line, second line or third line, and how I long for the days when it was Elmer Lach at center, The Rocket on right wing and Toe Blake on left wing.

I just asked one of my colleagues at *The Detroit News*—an avowed hockey fan and much younger than myself—if he could name five coaches in the National Hockey League. He named four, including Scotty Bowman of the Detroit Red Wings.

I still enjoy the games, but I wonder what's going on when they play baseball almost until Halloween, football into February, hockey into the middle of June and basketball near the end of June. Is there no letup? How much money do they need anyway? I know I couldn't afford to take my family to many games, and I have a pretty good job and make a nice salary. Two playoff games in Maple Leaf Gardens cost me $60 a ticket, or $240 for my two grandchildren, and the only reason I was able to buy them is that I happen to be in the sports writing business.

I know my feelings are not too popular. Our fans of today can't get enough of these sports—in person or on the tube. I think the NFL could play pro football the year round and still do well at the gate, and certainly in the TV ratings. So, I am a voice in the wilderness.

The thing that bothers me more than anything else is the way the fans are intruding on the games. TV has done this, but you can't blame TV. It is not their fault they are so good at what they do. They make all these games seem glorious beyond belief, and people with little else in life want to get in on the action.

And how do they do it? By misbehaving.

When I was a kid, I was a big Yankee fan. When Joe DiMaggio smacked a home run, everyone stood up and applauded and then they sat down. Today, the fans don't like to sit down. That's because you can't see them too well. At this last World Series between the Yankees and Braves, I had to move out of my seat in the auxiliary press box in Yankee Stadium because I couldn't see. The fans wouldn't sit down. It is vogue to stand when a pitcher has two strikes on a batter. The fans are trying to force a third strike. But the ones in front of me—not all, but enough—never sat down, and if you said anything to them all, they'd turn and give you some awful glares and terrible words. Who needs it?

Drinking is behind much of this behavior. Most teams will tell you they are concerned with the consumption of alcohol at their games and will point out that they shut down sales of beer at a certain time in the game—say, the eighth inning or the middle of the final period or quarter. Fine. What they don't say is that when they are dispensing beer, they put it into cups as large as barrels, and it doesn't take long for the consumers—the fans—to start getting tanked up.

And this, of course, helps the fans to lose control of themselves. They start yelling obscenities, throwing things or fighting with each other. They drink so much beer at the Red Wings' games in Joe Louis Arena that the lines to the men's room are especially long and many —anxious to get back to the action—urinate in the sink.

Once these people come through the turnstiles, they feel they have the right to act in any manner they wish—in ways they would never do at home or on their jobs. Bob Probert used to play hockey in Detroit and the fans went wild over him. The fact he was arrested so many times for drunken driving, and, finally, for possession of drugs, didn't matter. He may have been endangering the lives of others but it meant nothing to the fans as long as he could beat up somebody on the other team. And then the arena was filled with cries of "Probie! Probie! Probie!"

So you wonder where the class and the sportsmanship has gone. Forget it. It's not there anymore. It has been replaced by people who take these games very personally, as if they are part of them and believe they can have a direct effect on the ultimate outcome.

When the Baltimore Orioles met the Yankees in the playoffs, the fans got on Roberto Alomar for the way he spit at Umpire John Hirshbeck. They vilified him in ways that were shocking. They filled the air with their obscene chants—one dirtier than the next—and threw flashlight batteries at him on the field. (What kind of person would fill his pockets with flashlight batteries on the way to a ball game and know what he was going to do with them?)

I believe, like many others, that Alomar should have been suspended for the season, but the fans felt like they wanted to take the matter into their own hands. They cheered him in Baltimore, as if he was some kind of hero, and cussed him in places like Cleveland and New York, as if he was the devil incarnate.

So it didn't matter what he had done; just who he belonged to.

The saddest part of this episode was even though the fans in Yankee Stadium were all over the Baltimore second baseman with their filthy cries, the New York papers wrote the next day that Alomar was booed. Oh, really?

It is amazing how the fans look at these athletes. They are heroes to them and little else matters. The players make the fans feel good—instant gratification—and that's all that counts. When Keith Hernandez, first baseman of the New York Mets, came back from a drug trial in Pittsburgh where he admitted he broke the law for eight years by taking drugs, he was given a standing ovation by the fans in Shea Stadium. Knock one into the rightfield corner, Keith, and make us feel good. That was the extent of their values. I believe everyone should get a second chance but don't turn them into heroes; let them earn their way back.

The thing that's always asked of me, as a sports writer of more than 50 years, is: "Has the money spoiled the athletes?"

At first, I held out against this theory. I felt a man was a man was a man. No matter what he did—how much money he made—he would always revert to who he truly was; so I felt the money had no real effect on them. The good guys would still be the good guys, the bad guys still the bad guys. I've always felt that no matter how much you make—even millions—it doesn't change your personality. You are who you are and this will come out in time.

Besides, I felt no athlete wanted to look bad in public, so they always put their best efforts forward when they were playing.

Then I started changing my mind, and now I believe the money has had a terrible effect on the athletes. And I blame the agents. When they came on the scene, they told their clients to be wary of management. Management could not be trusted. So this created a very damaging gap. From the days when the players on the Tigers would drop in to see General Manager Jim Campbell and shoot the breeze with him before going to work, no player goes near the front office anymore—and the only time they see the officials of the Tigers is when they might be hanging around the edges of spring training.

All business goes through the agents, and you can only wonder what the players are thinking about when they carry cellular phones around with them and are talking into them when they're in the dressing rooms, on team busses and at the hotels.

The agents then told the players to be careful of the media. You can't trust those guys in the press. Then, it was the fans. Be careful around them, too, because we can make money out of them by selling them things, like autographs. Finally, the players were cautioned to be careful of each other.

So, an atmosphere of distrust has been created. From the days when the Tigers (Norm Cash, Al Kaline, Bill Freehan, Denny McLain, Willie Horton, Gates Brown) would hang out with each other, drinking, going to dinner, having family picnics and playing golf on off days, to the players of today going separate ways. If there are 25 players on the Tigers, 25 players go their own way after the games and don't see each other until the next day.

A nice way to create teamwork.

I can remember walking into the Tigers' dressing room years ago and sitting down and chatting with the players. They were always telling stories what happened at Elmira, what happened the last time a certain umpire worked one of their games, or even what happened last night in their personal lives. They held nothing back in my presence. They knew I knew the difference between what I could write—what I was privileged to—and what was off limits to me. It's not that I protected them; it was simply if what they were saying was personal, I had no right to it unless the ball club took some action against them and then would it become a story for me. Today, when I go into the Tigers' dressing room, the only way I can get anything from the players is if I have questions for them. Some days my questions aren't so good and some days their answers aren't so good. Gone are the days when I could capture the romance of this sport through the anecdotes of the players—the stories they told about themselves and their profession.

Yet, I still love my job, even if I don't love the games, the athletes or the travel as much as I used to. I have never socialized with the athletes I've had to write about. I don't go to their houses, and they don't come to mine. We don't play golf or go to dinner together. I like many of them, but I believe a professional relationship is the best way to go. I can be friendly, but I can't be their friend. This has been difficult to do because I have great admiration for men like Gordie Howe, Ted Lindsay, Dave Bing, Lem Barney and many, many others. It is a price you must pay to retain your integrity.

What I like most about my job is the writing, and how fortunate I have been to go to places like Wimbledon, The Masters, the British Open, Olympics in Mexico City, Montreal, Munich, Lake Placid, Sarajevo, Calgary and Albertville. I have covered 40 World Series, 15 Super Bowls, 20-25 Kentucky Derbies and Indy 500s. What has surprised me is that I thought I was a four-sport man (baseball, football, basketball and hockey) but I have liked the "events" better than the team games. I have loved the U.S. Open in ways that even I don't fully understand, and I'm talking about the U.S. Open in golf and U.S. Open in tennis.

I admit my interests have changed. I am not very interested in all the games, only the ones which concern us in Detroit. I don't care who the cornerbacks are for the Denver Broncos, or the small forward for the Utah Jazz. I keep up with the Green Bay Packers, Chicago Bears and Minnesota Vikings because those are the teams the Lions have to play. In hockey, I follow Toronto, Chicago and St. Louis because they are in the Red Wings' division—and it's the same in baseball: I keep track of the Yankees, Red Sox, Blue Jays and Orioles because they are the teams the Tigers must beat out, but, oddly, the only team I follow avidly in pro basketball is the Chicago Bulls of Michael Jordan. He is the finest athlete of our time and I am confounded when people in my town don't know this and get on his case because he was the one who stopped the Detroit Pistons' streak at two straight NBA titles.

What makes my job so fulfilling is I can write about all the things I see, hear, touch and feel. The guys on the city side go in after the crime or after the fire. I see everything as it is happening, and this, I believe, creates the best forum for writing (even if the guys on the city desk always laugh at us and think we work in the toy department).

Writing is like playing golf. No matter how well you play a round, you could have done it better. There is always a shot in there that could have been made better. The same with writing. No matter how well you may have written something, you could have written it better.

What's so marvelous is the next day you get that chance. You can never achieve perfection, but it sure is fun trying.

I have worked for The Associated Press in New York and Detroit and also for *The Detroit Times*, *Detroit Free Press* and *Detroit News*. My wife says all I have left is the Shopping News and I am out of here. I live in Clarkston, Michigan, about 45 miles north of Detroit, and treasure my home, my dog, Meka, and our four cats, Mena, the mother, and her three children, Boomer, Kugel and Kiki. I like college football the best—going to Ann Arbor and East Lansing for the games—but my favorite assignment has been the Kentucky Derby, and I still don't know what a furlong is. I have seen many sports in many places but still must make it to Monte Carlo for the Monaco Grand Prix and Hanover, New Hampshire, for a Dartmouth football game, when there is snow on the ground next to those red brick buildings and, even though I don't drink, a hot buttered rum by the fireplace at the local tavern.

I have never been bored one day in my job. Who could ask for more? (Well, an interview with Kim Novak wouldn't be bad, but then, that's another sport.)

Chapter 1:
The Kid

The first time I met Ted Williams he was screaming at me. It was just the two of us, The Ogre and me, in the Boston Red Sox's clubhouse in Fenway Park. Everyone else had gone home except Johnny Orlando, the clubhouse man and long-time friend of Williams. He kept glaring at me with that he-ain't-gonna-talk-to-you look on his face. Frankly, I was scared stiff.

It was 1956, my rookie year as a baseball writer, my first trip to Boston. It had been a wild day. Jim Bunning, a young righthander who threw from the side, pitched for the Tigers and, incredibly, struck Williams out three times. Nobody could ever remember that happening before.

But what did I know? I thought it would be a good idea to talk to Williams because he seemed to be the story of the day.

This was in the days when Williams was warring with the Boston press. Some of the writers—especially Col. Egan of the *Boston American*, a tabloid—were all over him, criticizing him at every turn, nailing him every chance they could get. Tempestuous Ted was an easy mark. He played his part by not talking to them, or snarling at them—even spitting at them. Not very nice but very compelling reading.

So I sat there in the Boston clubhouse, waiting, waiting, waiting for The Great Man to make an appearance. He was in a back room somewhere, maybe the trainer's room or the shower room—I didn't know. I just knew he wasn't there and was probably fuming over what had happened, but I kept on waiting. Soon, all the players were dressed and gone and it was just me and the ever-threatening Johnny Orlando, who was making all kinds of noises—grunts mostly, aimed at me—as he went about his chores, picking up laundry from the floor, putting shoes away and hanging up some of the shirts and pants.

Anyway, here he was—finally—coming out from the back of the clubhouse. Williams took one look at me and yelled: "WHO THE HELL ARE YOU? WHAT DO YOU WANT IN HERE?" He liked to talk in capital letters.

I identified myself, saying I was from *The Detroit Times,* and before I could go any further, he boomed, "Who cares? You're not supposed to be in here!"

"I just want to talk to you for a few minutes."

"Yeah! About what?"

"I wanted to ask you about Jim Bunning, the kind of pitcher he is."

Williams got a curious look on his face. "Oh," he said. "Sure. Sit down. Let me get another towel and we'll talk."

Talk? He talked for a half hour, maybe 40 minutes. He was charming and delightful, and I was stunned. I did not know my job yet but I knew something very special was happening. The Great Man was—in this instance—being a great man.

And now it is a lifetime later. Ted is in his 70s and I am in my 60s and while I have never socialized with the people I write about— the old professional bit—I still feel greatly honored that he has been very friendly for the past 40 years, and I am still awed in his presence.

Only a few athletes have ever done this to me. Ted Williams. Mickey Mantle. Joe DiMaggio. Three ball players, come to think of it. I have come to know the likes of Jack Nicklaus and Arnold Palmer, Gordie Howe and Magic Johnson, and while I have admired these men (I think every athlete should take "polite lessons" from them), I have never felt around them the things I have felt with Williams, Mantle and DiMaggio. I guess that makes me a baseball guy.

I am not dropping names here. But when you write sports for 50 years, you go to a lot of places and meet a lot of people. Some seem greater than life itself. Ted Williams has been one of these people.

When the Red Sox trained in Winter Haven, which was about 20 miles from Lakeland, home of the Tigers, I would visit him every spring and write a column. It got to be a joke in my sports department: "Falls do his Ted Williams column yet?" I couldn't help myself. I was drawn to this man as I have never been drawn to anyone, and it's probably my ego at work, but I just loved talking to him. Because of my age, I could talk about Phil Marchildon, the Philadel-

phia A's pitcher, or Stan Spence, the Washington outfielder who became a member of the Red Sox—or Johnny Pesky, who batted ahead
of Williams and was always on base because they never wanted to
walk anyone ahead of The Great Man. Williams loved these sessions,
too, because not many were around who remembered him hitting
that loudspeaker in Shibe Park on the final day of the 1941 season
when he got all those hits and finished up with a .406 batting average.

Now, Williams was 76 and ailing. He had had a stroke and all
kinds of stories were going around about his illness. I knew I had to
see him again and so I drove from Lakeland to his home in Hernando,
Florida, which is on the western side of the state.

The dalmation came bounding to the back door to greet me.

"Easy, Slugger! Easy!"

The voice came from the living room. It was a soft voice, but
filled with command. The dog stopped in his tracks.

Slugger.

Who else would own such a dog but Ted Williams?

The Kid.

The Splendid Splinter.

The Slugger.

"I love this old guy," said Williams as the dog leaped into his lap
as he sat on the sofa. "When I first got him eight years ago, I said,
'What do I need something like this for?' Now, every night before I
go to sleep, I pray to God that he takes me before he takes Slugger
because there is no way I could live without him. Right, boy?"

The dog looked up at him, his eyes shining. He licked Williams
on the bottom of his chin.

So you don't think this has been a pretty good life, eh? I have
grown tired of some of the games, and certainly the travel. I figured
it out the other day. I've been to Baltimore, on assignment, more
than 100 times. That means landing at Friendship Airport more than
100 times. Minneapolis, 60 times. Boston, 80 times. (Did you know
the wall in Fenway Park is 37 feet, 2 inches high? Some guys get the
37 feet but they miss the two inches.) I have literally been all over
the world, and what's been so amazing is that I grew up with the
four major sports—baseball, football, basketball and hockey—but I
also learned to love golf, tennis, auto racing, horse racing, the Olympics, even sailing. I don't know the first thing about sailing but I do
know it is a very special sport because the only way the boat can go
fast is if everyone cooperates; I've been in two Port
Huron-to-Mackinac races and they have been the two most exciting

events of my life. I sailed with eight men each time and not once—not once, mind you—did anyone use a four-letter word or even a six-letter word. We all knew what they were and what they meant, but out there, with nothing but water and sky around you, they were not necessary. All that mattered was moving the boat forward and this was done with great diligence, understanding, passion and love. And, naturally, when it was all over, I wrote what a much better world it would be if all of us could conduct ourselves as those guys did out on the water. But, of course, it can't be. Once back on land, we tend to return to what we are—often selfish, caught up in nothing more than trying to climb as high as we can in life.

Fifty years of writing sports is not a record. It's not bad, but it pales next to someone like Shirley Povich of the *Washington Post*. He is in his 90s and still writes an occasional column. That means he has been at it for 70 years or more. Shirley has been married as long as he has been writing and I asked him how any marriage could last that long. He said, "It's simple. We've just taken it one decade at a time."

You can have your heroes and I can have mine. Do you know what it means to sit next to Jim Murray at a World Series and talk to him for three hours? I mention this not to drop names again, but you should know that this is a very special man. Jim has had more than his share of physical problems, including poor eyesight. For a while, he was all but blind. But now we're in the Oakland Coliseum for the World Series and they have us stuck behind the rightfield foul pole, trying to peer through the screen to see what was going on. I, of course, am bellyaching all over the place. Why hold writer card No. 5 in the Baseball Writers' Association of America if this is the kind of treatment they are going to give you? I could not see the ball and could not figure out what was going on. When someone made contact, I had to look at all the fielders at once to figure out where the ball was going, by which time the play was over and I lost the rhyme and reason for everything.

Mr. Murray never uttered a word of complaint. He simply sat there (sometimes with a radio in his lap) and seemed happy to be part of the scene, even though he could see very little at all, including the rightfielder just below us. He simply waited until the game ended and then outwrote us all.

So, I am really a sports writing guy, not so much a fan, and my heroes are numerous. No. 1 of all time was Dick Young of the *New York Daily News*. I kept my distance from him because I felt he was on a much loftier plane than I could ever achieve. He was a great reporter and a masterful writer and could dispense more information, as well as opinions, than anyone who ever took part in our profession. He was so good, the other writers did not like him. No matter how hard they worked, they could not match him, in style or substance, and so they would sit in their little groups in press boxes and shoot their arrows at him. Young never cared. He didn't even duck. He'd just clobber them in the next day's paper.

Whenever you'd ask someone who was their favorite sports writer, they'd invariably say, "Red Smith." I never bought it. Red was a bright man, an elegant man, a man who could handle the English language better than anyone. But I never felt he wrote for the people. Guys would name him because, somehow, if you named Red Smith, it would bring you honor and elevate you in ways you could not do on your own. Young wrote directly for the people, the subway riders of New York City. He understood his readers better than anyone else. He did not write down to them but wrote for them, at their level, and no one ever had trouble understanding what he was saying. I never knew him to write a dull story or column, and we're talking about 40 years of journalism.

As Dick got older, his politics changed. He became narrow in his thinking. He could not abide young people and favored bosses over workers. This gave his critics a chance to get at him. It didn't matter. He still spoke his mind. When Dick Young wrote it, you read it. You may not have liked it, but you could not stay away from his work.

Young wrote some terrific stuff. Probably his finest lead came at a time when the Brooklyn Dodgers were blowing the National League pennant and he wrote, "The tree that grows in Brooklyn is an apple tree."

Another time, outfielder Sandy Amoros dropped two fly balls to hurt the Dodgers and all the writers came down on him. The next day or so, Amoros cracked two home runs in Ebbets Field and Young wrote, "Sandy Amoros dropped two more fly balls today—both into Bedford Avenue."

When Don Larsen, a man of loose-living habits, pitched his perfect game for the Yankees against the Dodgers in the 1956 World Series, Joe Trimble of the *New York Daily News* wrote one of the great leads of all time: "Don Larsen may be alcoholic but he'll never be anonymous."

Wonderful. But unprintable.

By the time the desk at the *Daily News* looked at Trimble's lead, Trimble had gone home. Young was still around working on his column. They called and asked if he could write a sub lead. No one could match what Trimble had done but Young came close: "The imperfect man pitched the perfect game."

I have other heroes, some of whom you probably don't know, but all were great men in my mind and did much to shape my life: Ted Smits, Will Grimsley, Murray Rose and Jack Hand of The Associated Press (where I broke into the business), Sam Greene and Hal Middlesworth, my rival writers when I started covering the Tigers in Detroit (both taught me how to behave myself on and off the field), Ed Hayes, Hal Schram, Jim Eathorne, Bill Brennan, all Detroit newspapermen.

Tom Gage, our baseball writer at *The Detroit News,* said to me one day in the press box: "How many ball games have you seen in your life?"

"Come on, Tom."

"No, really. How many?"

How could I count them all? I grew up in New York City when there were three teams—the Yankees, Giants and Dodgers. I was a nut. I went to a game every day in the summer. One of the teams was always at home, sometimes two, and if they played day and night, I'd see both games. The bleachers used to be 55 cents. I could come up with the dough very easily. My brothers taught me to go into Calvary Cemetery at the end of our street with a watering can, a trowel, a rake and pair of clippers. The cemetery would open at 9 a.m. and someone was always there visiting the graves. My brothers figured out they wouldn't be there at that hour unless they truly cared to be there and so when you approached them and offered to water their grave, they would always say yes. You'd put the trowel, rake and clippers on the ground and start hustling the water from out on the road, sometimes two or three blocks away. It didn't matter. As you raced back and forth, they would pick up the tools and start fixing the grave. They always gave you a dime, sometimes 15 cents, occasionally a quarter, and you had 65 cents in about an hour's time—55 for the bleachers and a dime for the subway, a nickel each way. Your mom always had two salami and tomato sandwiches ready to go in a brown bag and you were off and running, catching all the batting practice as well as the games in Yankee Stadium, the Polo Grounds and Ebbets Field.

"I've seen 5,000 ball games," I told Gage, counting my youth as well as my career as baseball writer and columnist.

He was holding a calculator in his hand and pressed some of the buttons.

"What are you up to?" I said.

"How many football games?" he asked.

My first game was at the Polo Grounds in 1937, the Green Bay Packers of Cecil Isbell and Don Hutson against the New York Giants of Mel Hein and Tuffy Leemans.

Tom asked how many basketball games, hockey games, Olympics, golf, tennis, horse racing, car racing—the works. He kept pressing the buttons.

"What the hell are you up to?"

He held up his hand for a moment, then looked at his calculator. He said, "Do you realize you've spent nine days of your life standing for the national anthem!"

Then there was the day in Fenway Park, going through the press gate, when the guard on duty said: "Writer number?"

I always said mine very loud so I could embarrass Tom, who is much younger and has a higher card.

"THIRTEEN!" I said.

The guard said, "Geez, that's a low number."

"Just think about it," I said. "If 12 guys die this year, I'll be No. 1."

The guard looked at me and replied, "Well, good luck to you!'

Chapter 2:
"Thank You, Mr. Sheary"

If you are in the newspaper business, is there anything more exciting than your first byline? Answer: No.

Mine happened when I worked for The Associated Press' sports department in New York City around 1950. I'd just been put on the staff and given a brand new title: Sports Clerk. More about this later. I was still a copy boy but now I could write and even put my name on stories.

The AP is a wire service which provides news to newspapers. The New York sports staff had 17 members. I was No. 17, the kid on the block. I didn't know very much—hadn't had much experience or even been to college. The boss was Ted Smits, the greatest boss I ever had—not a big sports fan but who made it all happen for me. He saw something in me that even I didn't see. Maybe it was my enthusiasm. Maybe my joy of sports. Or, maybe, because I could name the entire Philadelphia A's infield—Ferris Fain at first, Pete Suder at second, Eddie Joost at short and Hank Majeski at third (stuff he didn't know) plus the fact I was not afraid to use a broom to keep the sports department clean and ran coffee at an instant's notice, fetching it as quickly as possible, bringing it back the way each guy wanted it: black, black with sugar, sugar and cream, only cream. I memorized it all.

Anyway, he gave me my chance when I wasn't even ready to get a chance.

The AP had a weekly basketball poll, ranking the best college teams in the land. We would poll the writers on Monday, count the votes, and put the story on the wire for the Tuesday papers.

We served both morning and afternoon papers. The morning papers were called AMs, the afternoons PMs. We would alternate this story between the two cycles—first AMs, then PMs. Each cycle got a follow-up story.

Smits said one day: "I want you to do the follow-up story on the basketball poll for PMs."

He was very casual about it, but his words sounded like thunder in the skies, for this would be my first byline. Smart guy, Mr. Smits. He was not going to put any extra pressure on me.

The way it worked was this—whoever wrote the first story on the poll would start out this way: "Holy Cross, with a perfect 8-0 record, today was named the No. 1 college basketball team in the country by The Associated Press poll of sports writers."

Whoever did the follow-up story would say: "Holy Cross, voted the No. 1 college basketball team in the country by The Associated Press poll, will play Providence and Boston College this week."

My job was to do the second story.

From the very start, I did not know how to write. At the very, very start I could not link enough words together to make a simple sentence. More on this later, too. But I knew one thing: I did not want to do it the way it had always been done. I wanted to do it differently. Not to catch the boss's eye but because the one thing I always had, right from the start, even when I couldn't write, was ideas. My mind, for whatever the reason, was working all the time. Then, and even now. It is the one gift given to me.

I decided I would call the Holy Cross coach (whoever he was) and ask how it felt to be No. 1 in the country. Nobody had ever done this before and I thought it might make a nice story. At least a different story.

One problem: I didn't know how to do it and was scared stiff.

I knew I would have to find out where Holy Cross was and then find out the coach's name and get his phone number. I sure didn't want to do this in the office, because what if I failed? The other guys would look at me and see all my inexperience.

So I went home and asked my mom if I could make one long-distance telephone call. She, of course, said yes.

But I was still uptight. I didn't want her to hear what I was up to because, again, I might make myself look bad. I looked in a basketball book and found out that Holy Cross was located in Worcester, Massachusetts, wherever that was, and got the phone number from the long-distance operator.

I pulled the phone out onto our small front porch, yanking at the cord to make it reach, which it barely did, and then pulling the door closed on the cord until the door stuck on the cord. Later, I had trouble re-opening the door. But, finally, I felt safe enough to make the call.

I dialed the school and, speaking very softly, asked the woman who answered the name of the basketball coach and could I please speak to him.

"Yes," she said. "His name is Lester Sheary, but most people call him Buster. I'll connect you."

My breath was all but gone at this point and it didn't help when someone—a guy—picked up the phone and said, "Basketball office."

"Could I, uh, please speak to Mr. Sheary?"

"Speaking."

Now, my breath was gone, and along with it, my voice.

He said "hello" several times, wondering if anyone was on the line, when I managed to say, "Excuse me, but . . . I'm . . . very nervous."

He said, "Well, why don't you calm down. Take it easy. I'm in no hurry. Who am I talking to?"

I managed to tell him who I was and what I was up to and added, "Maybe I should call back later."

This man—whoever he was—was as kind as anyone I had ever encountered. He got me settled down, and then we spoke.

I said, "What does it feel like to be the No. 1 team in the land?" And, God bless him, he spoke for almost 15 minutes, teasing me along the way, getting me to laugh, getting me to relax.

I scribbled the notes and thanked him, and he said, "Hey, Joe, if you need anything else, you've got my number. Call again."

Well, I wrote the story, putting his quotes at the top, and the next day (I was told) Mr. Smits read the story and said, "I'll be damned . . . we've got all these big writers around here and this kid has the presence to call up the coach and talk to him."

That night, when I went to work, there was a note of congratulations from Mr. Smits in my mail box, with a paragraph that said, "Why don't you try a 'Sunday Special' this week? We'd like it by Thursday so we can move it on the wire by Friday."

More panic.

What was a "Sunday Special?"

I went to Will Grimsley, who ran the night desk, and showed him the note. He said, "Ted wants you to write a feature story for the Sunday editions, where they have a lot of room. You can let the story run."

"What should I write about?"

"Anything you want. I'll help you if you want."

I couldn't enjoy my moment of fame because now I had to produce another story. But, about what?

I went home and did not sleep very well. It hit me in the middle of the night. The baseball salaries were just starting to take off—Joe DiMaggio had received a $100,000 contract from the Yankees and Ted Williams got $125,000 from the Red Sox. That was it. I would pick an all-star team of the players making the most money at each position. This has been done many, many times in recent years but nobody—at least to my knowledge—had ever done anything like it before.

I knew my sports, even if I didn't know how to put it down on paper, and I spent the rest of the night coming up with my list. I had an old Remington typewriter at home and tried to put the story together but it was pretty much of a jumble.

That night I showed Will what I had done and he said: "Here, let me see what I can do with it." He wrote the most glorious first paragraph I had ever read in my life, especially since my name—"By Joe Falls, Associated Press Sports Writer" was at the top of it:

NEW YORK, Dec. 17 (AP)—It would cost $545,000 to field baseball's "Gold Dust" team, composed of the nine highest salaried players at each position."

He handed the paper back to me and said, "Now you finish it."

Finish it? It was easy after that. He got me into it and I just wrote down everything I knew. His phrase—"Gold Dust" team—was golden. It seemed as if every paper in the country picked up on it and used it in their headlines, mostly at the top of a page, eight columns wide. When these papers came into the office and Smits saw they all used the story with that headline, he said again, "I'll be damned."

Another note of congratulations. I never told him the phrase was Will's idea.

So, how does all this sports writing stuff get started? I'm not sure because I wasn't trained for it. It just happened.

Hockey tickets were at the bottom of it all.

I went to an all-boys Catholic School in lower Manhattan, just on the edge of the Bowery section. We lived in Queens and I went to LaSalle Academy because my father was a policeman in that district and knew something about the school. The tuition, as I recall, was $10 a month.

I got terrible marks. Not because I was dumb; I just wasn't interested in school. I was caught up with sports—playing in the streets and going to all the games—and I never studied or paid attention in class. I kept writing out lineups of the various teams and drawing pictures of old ball parks.

They graded you 0 to 100, with 65 a passing grade. In my junior year I failed three of six subjects: algebra, physics and history. I failed history because I put the correct answers on the wrong page and Brother George, the history teacher, gave me a 55. That was bad enough, but I got 19 in algebra and 47 in physics. I had to go to summer school, where I passed history easily enough but could only bump my physics grade to 49.

I was so far behind that in my senior year they had to put me into a special class with four or five other guys and give us two snap subjects—bookkeeping and typing—so we could earn our degrees. You needed 16 points to graduate. I got 16 1/4, so I was prepared for exactly nothing when I got my degree.

It was at LaSalle Academy where I achieved my most memorable athletic achievement. They always had a field day during the first week of school, holding it at a park down by the East River. It was a way of bringing everyone together and introducing new students to the school.

I was a freshman and you had to sign up for at least one event. I didn't want to sign up for anything, but chose the 100-meter dash because I thought it would be over the quickest and I'd be out of there.

I also could run pretty well.

But, at this age—14 and growing—I did not know about some of the finer requirements of athletic endeavor. Like jock straps. They gave us these tight-fitting uniforms—white shirts and white shorts— and, how shall I put this, they gave me a very small pair of shorts and I could not quite hide the bulge.

I was so embarrassed I hid in the bushes until they called my heat, then ran out sort of sideways to keep things to myself, and got down in starting position. Nobody seemed to notice anything.

Bang!

We took off and guess who bolted to the front? Guess who was 10 yards ahead of anyone else? Guess whose . . . well, you know . . . popped out of his shorts halfway down the track? Guess who struggled to shove it back in and finished 20 yards ahead of anyone else?

Brother George, a different Brother George who was the track moderator, stood at the finish line and I could hear him murmur as I ran by: "My word."

He came up to me later and announced, "That was a very impressive performance, Mr. Falls. As of Monday, you are on the track team. Please report back here at three o'clock in the afternoon."

When I was finished with high school, I went to work in the stock room of an insurance company in mid-Manhattan and it was OK until I found out that some of my friends had gotten jobs as copy boys at The United Press and were getting free hockey tickets from the sports writers. Talk about getting jealous. I didn't know what The UP was—but free hockey tickets! What was I getting in my stock room job? I could take home a few boxes of pencils, a few pens, and some carbon paper, but that was it.

One day, while riding the subway to work, I was looking through the job wanted section of the *New York Times* when I came across a two-line ad: "Wanted: Mail Boy. The Associated Press. 50 Rockefeller Plaza. $24 wk."

My heart leaped. In all of my infinite wisdom, I thought, "If they can get free hockey tickets at The UP, maybe I can get free hockey tickets at The AP."

I applied and was hired on the spot by Mr. Ken Nugent, who was, at this moment, the greatest man I had ever known. We talked a little sports and he smiled when he found out how much I knew.

I lugged mail around the executive office on the seventh floor and loved every minute of it. I had not been to the newsroom floor, but I knew where it was—down on the fourth floor—and that was close enough. I used to fill in for the receptionist on the executive floor—Hartrice Minturn (or Min)—and I loved that woman and got the thrill of my life one day.

It was very quiet on the executive floor. The carpeting was plush, all the office doors were closed, and hardly a sound was ever heard. The big boss was Kent Cooper, general manager of The AP. I'd see him occasionally as he waited for the elevator, saying, "Good morning, Mr. Cooper." He'd shrug, mutter something, and be on his way.

One day I was sitting at Min's desk when this man got off the elevator. He was neatly dressed in a suit and tightly knotted tie. He was carrying his hat in his hands.

"Excuse me," he said. "I have an appointment with Mr. Kent Cooper."

"May I have your name, please?"

"Lindbergh. Charles Lindbergh."

I nearly dropped the phone but got the call through to Mr. Cooper's secretary and followed Mr. Lindbergh with my eyes as he walked down the long hallway to the executive offices.

Then it happened. One day I was asked to take something down to the fourth floor and was stopped in my tracks. The noise was deafening. They had teletype machines all over the place, each clacking away, and people were rushing around in every direction, some calling across the room to someone else, some just yelling at no one in particular. I was stunned but exhilarated by the whole scene. So this was what newspapering was about. I asked for a transfer, from mail boy on the seventh floor to copy boy on the fourth floor, and got it very quickly.

But I was not quite in seventh heaven.

I spent most of my time working in the general news department. Over there, in the corner, looking out at the ice rink in Rockefeller Center, was the sports department. That's where I wanted to be. I wanted to be there so much that I was intimidated by that corner spot. I didn't dare go near it.

They had two copy girls working in sports—Helen in the daytime and Mickey at night. They were holdovers from the war when the guys went away to fight. As luck would have it, Helen got pregnant and quit and I got her job. Then Mickey got pregnant and quit and I got her job. As I've said over the years, I had nothing to do with either circumstance; I was just lucky it happened.

When I went to work for Mr. Smits in the daytime, he found out I could type and he had me do his letters. He would write them on his typewriter, then I would transfer them to office stationery with my typewriter. I figured this was secretaries' work, and so I would pile a lot of books around me when I was doing the letters so the other guys couldn't see what I was doing.

It didn't take long to figure out the real action was at night. Night baseball was in and what I wanted more than anything else was to work the Western Union ticker and take all the scores and type them out so they could put them on the wire. I got the chance when Mickey left and I was in my glory. My hours were 5:30 p.m. to 2 a.m., with Tuesdays and Wednesdays off.

Fridays were the best because everyone played at night on Fridays and I could handle all the games, inning by inning, pitching changes, home runs, the complete linescore, all nine innings, pitchers, catchers and home runs. I also handled linescores of the International League and American Association. Sometimes the ticker would not stop ticking and the tape would roll out in a never-ending stream. I had to type as quickly as I could, never making a mistake, because they took the scores out of my hand and put them on the wire without looking at them. I never made a mistake.

By now, I was starting to understand what was going on in the sports department and I got my first feelings that maybe I could be a sports writer.

I noticed they had a daily feature called "Sports Mirror." This was a look-back at sports—what happened five years ago, 10 years ago, 20 years ago and 25 years ago. The material came from a cabinet filled with diaries. It was the job of the sports editor to record, in brief, the happenings of that day in very simple terms. I watched how the guys would pull these books out and turn to the proper pages and copy that day's top event in one or two lines. I also noticed it was a chore for them to haul out four books and put them back.

I decided I would help.

I found the proper four books and typed, word for word, an entry from that day. I gave it to the night desk man and he couldn't be more pleased.

"Very good, Joe. Keep it up."

So, each night, I copied a "Sports Mirror." And then I decided I would do a whole week of them, and they were even more pleased. I figured if they liked one week, I would do two weeks, then a month, then two months. When I was something like 125 Sports Mirrors ahead, they said: "Uh, we've got enough for a while, Joe. Why don't you do something else?"

I used to open all the out-of-town papers. These came in by the hundreds. It was dirty work and my clothes would get filthy handling all the papers. I started bringing old clothes to work and putting them on when I had to open the papers—again trying to hide from everyone (especially the copy girls) because I looked so ragged.

I noticed *The Christian Science Monitor* out of Boston used "Sports Mirror" every day. My "Sports Mirror." I was startled, then pleased, to see my "work" in print. I started cutting them out until I had a whole notebook filled with "Sports Mirrors." I showed them to my mother and she was very proud of her son. I did not tell her the words weren't mine, just the typing. Still, I was thrilled. I knew what I wanted to be.

As time went on, they started giving me small assignments—a small college basketball game here, a boat race on the Hudson River there . . . things they did not want to waste their regular staffers on. I became what was known as a "stringer."

Pro basketball was such small potatoes in those days that nobody wanted to cover the 1952 NBA finals between the Minneapolis Lakers and New York Knicks. They gave the home games of the Knicks to me: 150 words and a box score. The games weren't even played in Madison Square Garden. The circus was in town and the Knicks got kicked out and played at the 69th Regiment Armory on

Lexington Avenue. I covered it all—those great Laker players, George Mikan, Jim Pollard and Vern Mikkelson, against the Knicks of Ray Lumpp, Carl Braun, Harry Gallatin, Vince Boryla and my main man, Dick McGuire. I got $15 a game.

My first stringer assignment was a swimming meet at Brooklyn College: 100 words and summaries. Spike Claassen, the assistant sports editor, wrote a note introducing me, saying I was there for The AP and would they kindly help me with the results. I was impressed and so was my mother. She dressed me in my Sunday best and I took the subway to Brooklyn and got completely lost. It took a while to find the school and by the time I got there, the program was half over. I knew I had to get down on the floor of the pool (that's what Spike told me to do) and talk to the coach and tell him what I needed. I wandered around looking for some stairs and wound up in the Brooklyn College dressing room. I asked where the pool was and they told me it was through that door at the far end of the room. Before they could say more, I went bursting through the door and wound up in a wading pool up to my knees . . . and there I stood, in top coat, jacket, pants and shoes, looking like an utter fool to the fans in the stands. As I danced out of the water and started across the pool in search of the coach, they gave me a standing ovation.

The union at the office noticed I was getting these assignments and told Smits that if I was good enough to go out and work for The AP, I should be put on the staff. I pleaded with them not to press the matter because I wasn't ready to go on the staff—this was my learning period. The union remained stubborn and Smits finally had to stop all assignments, and I was crushed. I figured my career was over before it started. How could I ever learn?

Mr. Smits did not rest. He called a special meeting with the union leaders and got them to agree to a new job classification— Sports Clerk. That meant if I did my copy boy chores to everyone's satisfaction, I could do some writing and editing in any extra time. The union agreed to the deal. I wanted to hug Mr. Smits but thought better of it. (Years later, at the Mexico Olympics in 1968, my old boss got a little high and I ran into him in the press room at about one o'clock in the morning. He was not a man given to mushy comments but that night he said: "You are the finest thing that's ever happened to me in my life.")

I knew what he was saying. He had lost a son through suicide and had to live with that terrible memory for many years. Somehow, I became something of a surrogate son and it took a little drink to tell me. That may have been the finest moment of my life.

When I became a Sports Clerk, my hours remained the same—5:30 at night until 2 o'clock in the morning. That was a joke. I was in there at three o'clock in the afternoon getting my copy boy chores out of the way so that by 5:30 I was ready to be a fulltime editor. I stayed until 6 a.m., four extra hours, when the wire closed. I was working 15-hour days that seemed like two-hour days. I loved every minute of it. I watched everyone, what they did and how they did it, and the light slowly started going on.

Sometimes very slowly.

I noticed the New York newspapers would arrive in our office starting at 8 o'clock at night. There were eight papers in those days—four AMs and four PMs. We got the *Herald Tribune* first, followed by the *New York Daily Mirror, News* and *New York Times*. The guys would look through the sports sections and anything we didn't have, they would pick up and rewrite and put it on the wire.

The nightside guys would go to dinner at about 7 o'clock, in time trusting me with the department. It wasn't that big of a deal because they usually ate downstairs and I could get them in a matter of minutes.

I waited for the night when they would not come back on time and we'd get one of the papers and I'd look through it for an item we didn't have and I would rewrite it and put it on the wire myself and they would be proud of me when they got back from dinner.

It was past 8 o'clock one night and they hadn't returned and the *Herald Tribune* was brought to the sports department. My big chance. I went straight to the sports section where they had a story saying that Phog Allen, the famed Kansas basketball coach, was named to head the West squad for the annual East-West charity basketball game in Madison Square Garden.

I went to the typewriter and started doing the story.

I wrote, "Phog Allen . . . "

The *Trib* had called him famous. But I wanted my story to be better than their story. I paused and wondered what was the next degree of famous, and quickly typed: "Phog Allen, infamous Kansas basketball coach . . . "

I put the story on the wire and immediately the bells started ringing from the other bureaus along the line.

"NY Sports. What mean 'infamous' first graph Allen story (SP122)?"

"NY Sports. Please re-read first graph Allen story (SP122). What mean 'infamous.'"

"NY Sports. Do not understand 1st graph Allen story (SP122). Please fix."

Guess who walked into the sports department at that moment? I froze in fear. What had I done? I still didn't know what "infamous" meant but it must have been something bad. The guys looked at all the messages, then at me, and broke up laughing. They were good to the kid. Very good.

Another time, Ed Corrigan, one of the staff writers in sports, was having a feud with Smits and he would fix him by leaving his byline off his stories. It was pretty childish and everyone laughed about it. On July 4, Corrigan was asked to write the AMs baseball roundup and he did, leaving his name off. I was running the wire and it was my job to edit his copy. I wrote in a byline: "By F.O. Corrigan" and I'm sure you can figure what the F.O. stood for. I intended to remove the byline but a guy said, "Joe, phone. It's for you." When I stepped away, the teletype operator picked up the copy and sent it on the national sports wire—baseball roundup by F.O. Corrigan.

When I saw it on the wire, I saw—once more—the end of my career.

"Kill it" I said, and the teletype operate stopped punching his keyboard and wrote "kill" under the story. I was in another panic. I went around to all the other departments—city desk, foreign desk, local, radio, even the photo department—ripped off the copy and threw it into the waste baskets. I hoped Mr. Smits wouldn't see it when he came to work in the morning. But surely, somebody would see it from another bureau and mail it to him.

I held my breath.

One day.

Two days.

Three days.

Nothing happened, except I decided never to fool around on the job ever again (a promise I have broken many times).

All was not so bad.

I was at home one day in 1951 when the phone rang. It was Ted Smits. He said, "You're covering the World Series today. Murray Rose can't make it. It is Yom Kippur and he has to stay home. Come by the office and I'll give you your press credential."

World Series? Yankees vs. Giants? The Polo Grounds? I had to sit down and get it all straight in my head. What would I do? How would I do it? I had never covered a baseball game in my life.

Mr. Smits gave me my credential and told me to write a 300-word sidebar on the New York Giants' dressing room.

When I got to the press box in the Polo Grounds, I went straight to Will Grimsley and told him of my dilemma. I asked what a sidebar was and he said it was easy to do—just go the Giants' dressing room and write down what they say and make a story out of their quotes.

Will said, "When the game is over, some of the writers will go to the Giants' dressing room. Just follow them. You don't have to ask any questions. Just listen to what's said and come back here and I'll help you with the story."

Great. The Giants were beaten 13-1 and now I was following the writers around the Polo Grounds to the Giants' dressing room in deep centerfield. There were only seven or eight of them, not the hordes we have these days.

We went into the dressing room and Leo Durocher, the manager, was sitting on a chair in the middle of the room. The writers gathered around him but nobody said anything. I stood one row behind them. In fact, I was the whole second row.

Durocher had the lineup cards on each of his thighs. He'd pick up one, tear it in half, then pick up the other and do the same. He'd replace them on his legs, tearing them in half again, and again, until the pieces got so small he couldn't tear them at all. That's when he started cursing.

Still, nobody spoke a word—not a single question, not a single answer. Finally, the writers drifted away and I was there, alone, with Durocher looking up at me. I looked down at the lineup cards, the tiny piles still neatly arranged on his legs, but didn't say anything. He just kept staring at me until I, too, left.

When I got back to the press box, Will asked, "Well, what happened?"

"Nothing," I said.

"What do you mean nothing? What did the players say? What did Durocher say?"

"I didn't talk to the players and Durocher didn't say anything."

Will stared at me. "You don't have any quotes?"

"I don't have any quotes."

Now he looked around, slightly exasperated. "Tell me what happened—what did you see in there?"

I told him about Durocher and the lineup cards, the way he kept tearing them in half until he couldn't tear them anymore, getting madder and madder by the moment.

"Write that!" Will said.

"Write what?"

"What you saw. Exactly as you told it to me."

I sat down at my typewriter and before I had six words on the paper, I had to ask the teletype operator how to spell "solemn." He told me and I thanked him. I also told myself that as long as I lived, I would never forget how to spell this word—and I haven't. I knew I had to get something out of this day, especially if my boss was going to get mad at me.

I was writing a quote story without quotes.

Smits, back in the office, saw what I wrote—a piece about a very delicate moment—and for the third time, he said: "I'll be damned."

He sent me back again the next day, when the Series switched back to Yankee Stadium, and told me I would do the notes.

I asked Will: "What does he mean, notes?"

"Forget it," said Will. He wrote the notes that day and put my name on the story. It was easier for him. It gave him more time to do his own work.

Will covered a lot of basketball in those days—he and Ben Phlegar used to work the tournaments in Madison Square Garden: NIT and NCAA. They both liked me and brought me along to do the box scores. So there I was, at courtside, for the biggest games of the year while my buddies were up in the balcony or at home watching on TV. A long ways from wanting free hockey tickets.

The NIT was the big tournament in those days. The top four seeds were eliminated in one day and Kentucky was victim of the biggest upset. The Wildcats came in as the No. 1 team in the nation, unbeaten in something like 22 games. They had some fabulous play-ers—Ralph Beard and Alex Groza among them.

Loyola of Chicago, with Jack Kerris at center, was giving the Wildcats all they could handle and wound up beating them. Groza, Kentucky's All-America center, fouled out with a couple of minutes to go. Will was furiously into his lead, writing about this big upset, when I noticed Groza crying on the bench, with a towel pressed against his face.

You never interrupted Will when he was writing because he was so deeply into it that he would get rattled and then you would get rattled.

But I felt I had to talk to him.

"Will. Look at Groza. He's crying."

Will took one look, pulled the paper from his typewriter and started all over. He wrote about Kentucky losing and the heartbreak it created for its great center, Alex Groza. It was not until years later we found out why Groza was crying. Kentucky was shaving points that day and the Wildcats shaved them too closely and lost. This was in the middle of the great basketball scandal of the early 1950s—a point-fixing scandal that pulled down the sport in New York and many parts of the country.

Many years after that, on a quiet Sunday afternoon in East Lansing, it all came back to me again. I'd been sent to Michigan State because there was some kind of racial problem on the team and I was to find out what was going on.

As I watched the team practice in Jenison Fieldhouse, I saw a man standing off in the corner, with his hat pulled down over his eyes, staring out at the players on the floor.

I thought back to that night in Madison Square Garden when they were playing the Red Cross game—the big one of the year, pitting the national champions against the industrial champions, in this case Kentucky of Groza and Beard against the Phillips Oilers of Bob Kurland and Jesse (Cab) Rennick. That was the night Beard—a marvelous player and an All-American—threw in seven straight set shots. They shot with two hands in those days and he nailed seven in a row.

I walked up behind this shadowy figure and leaned in close to the back of his head and whispered: "Red Cross game. Kentucky vs. the Phillips Oilers, seven straight set shots."

The man never turned around. He said softly, "Whoever you are, God bless you."

That's how I became friends with Ralph Beard.

Chapter 3:
"He shoots. He scores!"

Hockey has played a big role in my life. I grew up in Woodside, Long Island, in the Borough of Queens—just six subway stops from mid-town Manhattan. As I said, my father was a policeman and walked the beat in lower Manhattan. He earned $56 a week for what seemed like forever and we had everything—a house, a car, food and clothes. This was in the 1930s and 40s and our rent never changed. It was $30 a month because my mother's brother owned the house and did not have it in his heart to ever ask for more. My grandmother lived upstairs for free and so Uncle John never made a penny out of his investment and probably lost a lot.

All I did growing up—or so it seemed—was play hockey. To this day, I've never been on a basketball court and the only time I've ever taken a shot at the basket has been at Pistons' practices when the ball would roll to me and I'd put up one of my famous one-handers. It was famous because my effort never reached the basket and usually resulted in Bill Laimbeer laughing at me. Laimbeer laughed at me a lot, especially when I wrote about basketball.

I lived on roller skates from September until May, when it got too hot to play hockey, and we'd play softball all summer long, waiting for September to roll around again. We played on roller skates because we did not have any ice, and even if we did, nobody could afford ice skates anyway.

We would put on our ball-bearing skates and chase a roll of friction tape around (regular pucks were too heavy and didn't slide on the concrete), and it was all very serious business. We played in a YMCA league and the only reason we ever won a title—in 1945—was because all the guys were away to war and those who were left behind either were too young or not very good.

John King started it all.

I don't imagine anyone remembers his name but it once was headlines in the New York newspapers. That's when he was electrocuted for killing a man.

I was 11 years old or so and had never been on roller skates when I bumped into John King at the local candy store. (Candy store: That's where you bought tobacco, newspapers, magazines, soda pop, candy and comic books.)

He said, "What are you doing Saturday?"

"Nothing." You didn't make many plans at 11.

"Would you like to play some hockey?"

Hockey? I had no idea what he meant.

He said, "We're playing the Laurel Hill gang and we need some guys on our team."

"Sure," I said. "Where are we playing? What time?"

John King played on the Laurel Hill team and they'd had a big argument and he was going to start his own team and get even with them. I did not know it was going to be a grudge match.

I found some skates in the basement and an old stick in the corner and practiced up and down the street, until I went over to Laurel Hill for the game. We played under a bridge and it was tricky going because there was no way to stop the puck from going out into traffic. The game had to be halted while one of the players waited for the cars to pass and went out there and shot it back in. We took turns doing it, one team, then the other.

We had exactly six players. That's all John King could summon up. I don't remember who won or lost—except that King played like a demon, sweating, cursing, barging into everyone. I pretty much stood in front of the goalie as a defensive defenseman because I could not skate from one end of the rink to the other.

A few years later, John King and two pals—Richard Powers and Raymond Mallard—were caught stealing a car outside of a diner on Northern Boulevard in Queens. The owner had just come out of the diner and saw what they were doing and they shot him dead.

King disappeared and, a few days later, there was a headline on page one in the papers: "King Caught in Chicago."

I paid no attention to it because I did not think it was our John King. I didn't even know he had killed somebody.

But he was the one and all three went to jail, then to trial. King and Powers were sentenced to die in the electric chair at Sing Sing Prison while Mallard was given a life sentence.

Our whole neighborhood was frozen in fear, thinking of what was about to happen.

I remember the night. The execution was set for 10:30 and when I went over to the candy store to get the early editions of the *News* and *Mirror* (2 cents each) for my father and there, on page one, was a picture showing some people leaving a building and again I did not know what it meant. It was John King's family leaving Sing Sing Prison that afternoon after seeing him for the last time.

We used to sit under the street lights in front of my house arguing baseball. Who was the best centerfielder, the best shortstop—anything to get an argument going. On this night, we just sat there, not saying much. We knew when the switch would be thrown and when the time came, nobody said a word. I remember looking down at the pavement and seeing two ants. At least they were alive.

We went home without even saying, "See ya tomorrow."

But that's when my love for hockey was first kindled. I played until I was 18. It was all I ever did. I played after school, at night under the bridge, all day Saturday and Sunday. I never studied, never thought of anything else, even girls. The game consumed me. I lived to play for the Woodside Rangers, YMCA champions, 1944-45. I even got a goal in the championship game at Windmuller Park, a game witnessed by—well, I don't think anyone was there except us.

They were terrific days, especially Sundays. We'd play in the afternoon, then go to the New York Ranger games at night. If it snowed, we went to Madison Square Garden in the afternoon to see the New York Rovers of the Eastern League, plus a prelim game involving local teams: Jamaica Hawks, Sands Point Tigers, Manhattan Arrows and Brooklyn Armed Torpedoes, starring the hefty but hard-shooting Bill Sweeney.

We would repair to Broadway for a roast beef sandwich ($1.25) and be back for the Ranger game that night—a mere case of heaven on earth.

I was 12 years old when the guys in the neighborhood came to my house and asked my mother if they could take me to a hockey game at The Garden. I'd never seen a hockey game—and, at this age, was not allowed out of the house at night.

My mother wasn't sure this was a good idea.

"Aw, c'mon, Mrs. Falls. We'll take good care of Joe. We'll watch him all the way."

Finally she relented but made them repeat their promise that nothing would happen to me.

It was the Rangers against Toronto Maple Leafs, the winter of 1940. The game did not start until 8:30 but we left at 5 o'clock to get in line at The Garden. These guys had their own section in the balcony—Timmy Murphy's section. They got it for every game. It was important to have your own section because you could not see much from the second row. If you had the front row, you could lean over the railing and watch the game. The guys in the second row would climb into the front row and stand on the seats and lean on you so they could see, too. The guys in the third row would climb in behind them and get into the pile, now three deep. If you were in the front row, you could see well but you couldn't move. It felt as if your chest was going to cave in. But this is how it was done and nobody complained. These guys came from all over the city but they grew to know each other and all the discomfort was worth it.

It cost 50 cents to get in—30 cents if you had your General Organization card from school. When the gates opened at 6 o'clock, we'd race as fast as we could up the stairs, five or six flights, around and around, and dash to claim the front row seats. It was all pretty silly because this was Timmy Murphy's section and nobody was going to take it from him. He was 6-8.

The Rangers won, 3-2, and I can still see Lynn Patrick getting the winner on a backhander from the slot from about 30 feet out. He sent the puck whistling past Turk Broda, the Toronto goalie, and while the place went mad, the guys in our section started a rhythmic chant: "Broda has a hard on! Broda has a hard on!"

We got home at about 11:30, with my Mother waiting for us. You could see the relief in her face when she saw me. My first night out and I got home safely.

"He was fine—we had a good time, Mrs. Falls," the guys said.

After they left, I was still excited. "You should have seen it, Mom. The ice—all white. The uniforms. The crowd. The noise. The organ music. And guess what?"

She said, "What?"

"Turk Broda has a hard on."

How can I describe the look on her face? She sputtered, "Who said that? Who told you that?"

"The guys. They yelled it out when the Rangers got the winning goal."

"You go right to bed, you hear me! I don't ever want to hear you say that word again. Your father will speak to you in the morning."

I was confused. Baffled. Hurt. What did I say? What did I do wrong? At 11, the mysteries of life were—mysteries.

About a year later, I started going to all the games—25 a season. That's when they played 50-game seasons. The Rangers weren't very good. They'd finish last or next to last and never made the playoffs. They once lost 15-0 in Detroit. Two weeks later, again in Detroit, they were beaten 12-2. It didn't matter. The game was so colorful, so exciting, that I could not wait until the Rangers played again.

My favorite player was forward Bryan Hextall. Hex. He played on the first line with Phil Watson and Lynn Patrick. We would wait for them after the games, standing in the cold darkness outside the Garden. We never asked for autographs. You just didn't do it. It was enough to see them come out of that side door, smile once in a while, with their beautiful wives at their sides, and disappear into the darkness of 49th street. Life was never better than in those moments. Our heroes, close enough to touch.

The fans used to hang signs for the players, and I thought, "Heck, I'll make a sign for my man, Bryan Hextall."

I got a window shade, put it on some newspaper on the floor of our living room, and painted his name in red. It looked terrific. We had a seat cover factory at the corner of our street and I knew the people who owned it and asked them if they would punch rings into my sign so I could hang it from the balcony.

I could not wait until the night I could hang it up.

We got to Timmy Murphy's section and all the guys helped me with it. I raced around to the other side of the balcony to see how it looked and my heart sank. It was so small you could hardly read it.

I wanted to take it down out of embarrassment but the guys said, "Naw, leave it up. He'll like it."

When the Rangers came out for practice, I didn't want to look. The guys started yelling down to Hextall and shaking the sign. He looked up and waved his stick at us.

Heaven.

I tossed two pennies on the ice, which he picked up and put into his glove for good luck. He waved his stick again and smiled.

Heaven on earth.

Afterwards, I waited for him outside on the sidewalk. I wanted to ask him if he'd sign my sign. He came out and I saw a smile on his face.

"Mr. Hextall . . . I was wondering if you'd sign my sign?"

"No!"

I looked up at him.

His smile grew wider. "But I'll tell you what," he said. "You be here on this same spot next Sunday night at 7 o'clock and we'll see what we can do."

"Yes, sir. Thank you, Mr. Hextall. Thank you."

The next Sunday, at exactly 7 p.m. (actually, I was there at 5 p.m.) I saw his face from behind the door. A guard was standing with him. Hextall looked out, saw me, and pointed me out to the guard. The guard came out and said, "Mr. Hextall would like to see you inside."

I went through the door and he extended his hand and asked my name. He said, "Come on inside. I want you to meet some of my friends."

He led me into the Rangers' dressing room and my eyes smarted from the bright lights. I looked around and everything seemed to be spinning. I could see the players in front of their lockers or walking around the room but it was pretty much of a blur.

Hextall cried out, "OK, you guys! I want you to meet my friend, Joe Falls. Get over here and sign his sign."

One by one, the players came over—Neil Colville, Mac Colville, Alex Shibicky, Davey Kerr, Ott Heller, Phil Watson, Lynn Patrick, Muzz Patrick, Alfie Pike . . . the whole team. They all signed the sign, then shook my hand and smiled.

Heaven on earth? How could anything ever be better?

The guys in the balcony were astounded when I showed them the sign. Every player. Every signature. I hung up the sign one more time, then put it in my room at home. I mean, suppose somebody tried to steal it?

Years passed. Hextall retired. I got older. I became a sports writer. When he was named to Hockey's Hall of Fame, I took the train to Toronto (not on assignment) and stood in the back of the room during the ceremony.

I approached him when it was over, introduced myself and asked if he remembered the kindness he had shown to a 12-year-old boy in New York. He couldn't remember. OK. I swallowed that but told him how happy he had made me, and once more, he gave me that smile.

Soon, word came out of Western Canada that Hextall was ailing. The doctors had to remove one of his legs. Then there was more bad news. They had to remove his other leg. I could not imagine him not able to get around, not after the wonderful way he played for the Rangers.

I was covering the Detroit Red Wings and one day they gave us a press release saying they had obtained Bryan Hextall, Jr., from the Atlanta Flames. He would play the next night in Olympia Stadium.

I went out and bought a window shade and a can of red paint. I drew another sign, this time for Bryan Hextall's son. I hung it in front of the press box and waited for the players to come out for practice.

Young Bryan saw the sign immediately. He kept looking up as he skated around the ice. A sign in front of the press box? I was tempted to throw him a couple of pennies.

After the game, I went into the dressing room with the sign. I introduced myself to young Bryan and told him my story. He had the same smile as his dad.

"Now I want you to do me a favor," I said.

"What's that?" he said.

I picked up a pen and signed my name on the sign. "I want you to give this to your father and thank him for the kindness he showed to a young boy a long time ago."

Years later, when Ron Hextall, Bryan Hextall's grandson, played goalie for the Philadelphia Flyers, I told him the story and got a hug out of it. I'm not sure if Ron Hextall has hugged many sports writers in his time.

I was such a nut about hockey that I saw 125 Ranger games in a row—five full seasons. My streak was broken when my brother Buddy got married and I had to go to the wedding on a Sunday night. I was so mad I did not speak to him at his wedding, sitting in a side room by myself, refusing all condolences and even the food. I would make him suffer.

One night I saw goalie Chuck Rayner of the Rangers come out of the net and play the point on a power play—pads, goalie stick and all. I never laughed so hard in my life. It was a ludicrous scene but that's how much Rayner wanted to win. He probably was the only goalie to ever do such a thing and you could look it up. I just don't know where.

I could never get enough hockey. On Saturday nights we'd go over to Wally Weiman's house and listen to the games from Maple Leaf Gardens in Toronto—Foster Hewitt in the Gondola. None of us knew what a Gondola was but it sounded like the most magnificent place in the world. The sound would come in strong, then fade, then come back. We went to Wally's house because he was the only one with a radio that could pick up any of these games. He was the goalie on our roller hockey team.

I loved table games as a kid and I bought a "Lester Patrick Hockey Game" for $1.95. Lester Patrick was a player, coach and general manager of the Rangers, so this seemed like a very official game.

It came with a playing board divided into squares. You had a pair of dice—one telling you which way the puck should go—F for forward, L for left, R for right, LD for left diagonal and RD for right diagonal. The other dice told you how many squares to move the puck. The game had players painted on the board and if the puck passed over them, it went the other way. I played this game for hours on end, announcing everything as I went along. You always announced anything you played.

I had one problem with my announcing. I'd copy the lineups out of the *New York Times* and put them into a notebook so I would have an official record of everything that went on. The Montreal Canadiens had a player named Joe Benoit . . . and I would say things like: "Here's Ben-OIT" up the left sideboards, over to Lach, back to Ben-OIT, ahead to Richard . . ."

Fine.

But when I listened to the games they spoke of a "Joe BEN-wah." Who was "Joe BEN-wah?" I could never figure it out. And, in time, I forgot about it . . . until one day many years later when I was driving to Ann Arbor for a football game and was going through some woods in Plymouth, Michigan; then it hit me. Joe Ben-OIT and Joe BEN-wah were the same guy. The same player. I got hysterical. I could not stop laughing. I pulled off the road and called the sports department at the *Free Press* and told my friend, Jack Saylor, who was always a big man on names, what a dumb thing I had done. He laughed. I laughed. We laugh every time we see each other.

My Uncle Hans would watch me play this table game, rolling the dice furiously and broadcasting feverishly.

He said, "You like that game, don't you?"

"Yeah," I replied, "but there's one problem."

"What's that?"

"No red light. They light a red light when a goal is scored but I don't have one."

I was being pretty clever. I knew my uncle was good at fixing things. He could put in a red light for me.

"Let me see what I can do," he said.

The next day, there were two tiny red lights hooked up at either end of the board, with two sets of wires and two switches to turn them on.

"What do you think?" he asked.

"It looks great. But there's one other problem. They have a green light to signal the end of the period."

He looked at me and smiled. "Okay, two green lights coming up."

He installed them next to the red lights, added more wires and two more switches.

I said: "Terrific! But they sound a buzzer when the green light goes on . . . "

His smile turned to a look of dismay. "All right. All right. I'll see what I can do."

He delivered the buzzer in a few days. It looked like a small brass pill box. But darned if you didn't press a button and the buzzer buzzed and the green light went on at the same time.

"All set?" he asked.

"Not . . . quite. Before the games, they play the national anthem and I don't have a national anthem."

He didn't say anything this time but a few days later there was a record album on the dining room table featuring the national anthem played a dozen different ways. I got excited and cranked up the victrola and put the music on and stood at attention at the dining room table. My uncle saw this and the smile was back.

"Have a good time," he said, turning to leave the room.

"Thanks. But, uh . . . "

"What now?"

"The national anthem is fine, but when they play in Canada, they play the Canadian national anthem."

My uncle left the room without a word, never to attend another of my table games.

You can only imagine my delight when, years later, I was able to have lunch with the two great hockey announcers, Foster Hewitt in Toronto and Danny Gallivan in Montreal—luncheons that lasted hours and hours. I was not ashamed to tell them I loved them because I grew up listening to them. I even told them about Uncle Hans.

I was transferred from New York to Detroit when I worked for The Associated Press. My boss, Ted Smits, knew I was No. 17 on his 17-man sports staff and I could learn more, quicker, as a one-man operation in the Detroit bureau. He cared for me a lot and wanted me to go to Chicago to become the No. 3 man in that bureau. Old Charles Dunkley had retired and Jerry Liska and Charles Chamberlain moved up and I would work behind them.

I'd never been out of New York and was afraid to go to Chicago. I thought it would swallow me up. I told Mr. Smits I did not want the job, preferring the safety and security of New York, my old hometown.

Murray Rose, one of the staffers in the sports department, told me I had made a major mistake. "You never turn down another job offer," he said. He indicated I was finished with Mr. Smits.

A few weeks later Murray came back to me and said, "Hey, I hear the Detroit job is open. Why don't you apply for it?"

"I thought you said I was finished—Mr. Smits would never listen to me."

"Try him," Murray said. Murray was a good guy—no, a great guy. He cared for me, too. I didn't know it but a setup was in the works.

"Mr. Smits, excuse me. I know I turned down Chicago. I shouldn't have done that. But I understand you are looking for someone to go to Detroit and I was wondering. . . "

"When can you leave?" he asked. This was on a Friday.

"I don't know," I said.

"OK," he said, "Be on the train to Detroit Sunday night. They're waiting for you on Monday morning." (Do they have a Hall of Fame for bosses?)

I was still scared. What did I know about Detroit, Chicago or any place else? I took the train out of Grand Central Station, buying a *Detroit Free Press* to get some idea of what was going on in Detroit. This was a mistake.

I read a hockey story by Marshall Dann and a feeling of depression swept over me. He wrote a line that read, "Ted Lindsay scored on a five-foot kill."

I read that line again and again.

A five-foot kill.

I could never write that well, not in 9,000 years. I didn't sleep for one second on the train that night.

Yet, all I could think of was my first Red Wings' game in Olympia Stadium the following Thursday night against the Boston Bruins. Guess who I sat next to? Marshall Dann of the *Free Press*. He could not have been nicer. He welcomed me, told me it was good to have me around, and if there was anything he could do for me, just ask.

I thought of asking him where he thought up lines like "a five-foot kill" but didn't. Good move, Joe.

As the game unfolded, I couldn't get over Gordie Howe's shoulders—they were so massive. He almost looked like a gorilla in a red uniform. He scored a goal that night—and the move to Detroit suddenly didn't seem so bad.

Little did I know but a story was happening right at my side. The official scorer was Ross Jewell. I sat next to him and he sat next to Fred Huber, the publicity man of the Red Wings. Jewell was a nervous guy. He did not seem to enjoy the games. He was afraid of making a mistake in giving out the goals and assists. He would write the numbers of the players on a sheet of paper as each touched the puck. If someone scored, he would go back two numbers and give assists to those players.

He would always ask of no one in particular, "How did that go?" He needed all the help he could get.

Huber, a quiet, soft-speaking man, would say, "I think Gordie got the tip of his stick on the puck over the corner."

That was enough for Ross Jewell. He would give Howe an assist, whether or not he had written his number down on the paper. I don't know how often this happened, but it happened more than a few times. Howe hardly needed any help but he got it. Imagine if this story broke these days. Back then, nobody said a thing.

The Red Wings were good in those days. They were in the process of winning seven straight league titles. But that first year, they were beaten by the Bruins in the playoffs, even after winning the first game, 7-0, and so I was disappointed because I thought I was going to cover a Stanley Cup champion.

But they won the next two seasons, beating Montreal both times in the finals—one in sudden-death overtime when Tony Leswick fired one from the right boards which caromed off defenseman Doug Harvey's glove and past goaltender Gerry McNeil.

When you worked for The AP, the premium was on speed and accuracy. You had to get it right and you had to do it fast. But how could anyone prepare for a sudden-death game in the final game of the playoffs?

When Leswick scored, I rolled the copy very fast, very accurately, and while I didn't know it at the time, I was starting to become a newspaperman.

Jack Adams was the boss of the Red Wings in those days— roly-poly Jack. He could be as sweet as syrup or as nasty as thorns, depending on what mood was needed.

He was a dictator to the players. He'd go into the dressing rooms between periods and scream at them. He would throw orange slices at them to show his anger. And, always, he had a train ticket protruding from his pocket. That was to let them know if they didn't like what he said or what he did, they'd be on their way out of town in the morning.

Adams lived in Detroit, out by the University of Detroit, and his servant was named Joseph. Joseph was a smart guy. He'd listen for

Mr. Adams to return from the games on Sunday night. If his tires screeched as he turned into the driveway, Joseph would go upstairs and pretend to be asleep. He knew the Red Wings had lost. If he couldn't hear the tires, he knew they had won or tied and he would greet him at the door and say, "Welcome home, Mr. Adams. How did things go this evening?"

Adams was a generous man—almost too generous. He was forever wining and dining the writers, photographers and broadcasters. He would hire out entire restaurants and bring forth the best in food and drink. He was trying to buy the favor of these media types and was immensely successful. He had most of them in his hip pocket. Who could not be nice to Jolly Jack?

When the Wings won the Stanley Cup in my second and third years in Detroit, I was invited, along with my wife, to the victory party at Yeaman's Restaurant in downtown Detroit, where, again, the best of food and drink was available to all.

We drank champagne from the Stanley Cup for two straight years and my wife said to me: "How often do they have these parties?"

I said, "Every year, my dear. Every year."

Yeah. Sure. The Red Wings finally won again—42 years later.

Gordie Howe was the big player on the Red Wings. He was the best hockey player I ever saw. He could make more instinctively right moves in the course of one game than many players could in a month or two. Much has been made of his meanness on the ice. Howe could be tough, but what most people missed is that he was so low-keyed that he never played with the great abandon others did. Everything came so easily to him that he did not have to push himself. I always felt that if he had had the temperament of Maurice (The Rocket) Richard, he could have set records that would never be broken.

Gordie was a show by himself. Even when the Red Wings lost, you could go home with the knowledge you had seen a great artist at work. And there was no finer person—more thoughtful to others—than this man. He never understood his own greatness, and still doesn't.

I would get all kinds of letters saying such things as, "Dear Mr. Falls: I thought you ought to know this. I was struggling in my driveway during that blizzard the other day, trying to dig out so I could go to work, when this guy came along and said, 'Watcha up to?' I told him and he got a shovel and started working with me. It wasn't until we were done that I got a good look at him and it was Gordie Howe."

Or . . .

"Dear Mr. Falls: We were supposed to have one of the Tigers at our boy scout meeting the other night but he never showed up. One of the guys said, 'Hey, let's go over to Gordie Howe's house and see if he'll come out and talk to the kids.' Gordie was here in 15 minutes and saved the whole evening."

But, boy, was Howe a tough interview. He was the main story in most games but he did not like talking about himself. So you had to be ready for him. It just didn't do any good.

You'd walk up to his locker and the first thing he'd do is pin you to the wall with his shoulder, harder and harder, until it started to hurt. You didn't want to say anything because this was the great Gordie Howe.

He'd shove an elbow into your ribs—Ooof! That hurt, too, but not enough so you couldn't stand it. Then, and I was never sure how he learned to do this so perfectly, he'd grab the end of your penis through your pants and squeeze. Sometimes, he went for the testicles . . . so by now you thought better of everything and just left. He didn't smile so much as he'd leer.

One night, before a game, I went in to see him. Brooks Robinson had signed a $100,000 contract with the Baltimore Orioles. These deals were becoming commonplace and I said to Howe, "Why don't you ask for a $100,000 contract?"

He shrugged.

"No kidding, you ought to get more, and $100,000 isn't such a big deal anymore," I said.

"I'll think about it, " Howe said.

Howe was working for small bucks. It seemed like they gave him the same contract every year—$35,000 or so and a lot of nice words. Owner Bruce Norris would fly into town some time in June and Howe would be called into the front office to talk about the next season. All the Olympia Stadium execs would be on hand—Nick Londos, Lincoln Cavalieri and Lou Marudas, who was the publicity man.

The following August, I saw Howe at a charity golf tournament. He motioned me over.

"I want to thank you for what you did for me."

"What did I do?"

"My new contract—you're responsible for it."

I didn't know what he was talking about. I'd forgotten what I said to him.

Howe went on: "Norris came into town, like always, and they called and asked me to come in and see him. I parked in the lot next to Olympia and started up that long flight of stairs—the one that goes straight up to the front office. Halfway up, I thought of you and what you said." It came back to me now but I could not believe what I was hearing.

"When I went in there, Mr. Norris greeted me and said, 'How are things going, Gordie? I hope you're having a nice summer. I was wondering, what do you think about next season?'"

I caught my breath and said, "What did you say?"

"I told him, 'I want $100,000 next season,'" Howe replied.

"What'd he say?"

"He said, 'Fine. Sure, Gordie. Anything you say.'"

It is hard to tell this story because it smacks of self-promotion, but it happened, and I only relate it to you so you can understand the kind of man this is—quiet and humble, with no airs about himself at all. Gordie Howe is No. 1 on my list of all-time nice guys in sports.

Chapter 4:
Ebbets Field and Earthquakes

When I worked for *The Sporting News,* I wrote a column that I'd been in 37½ major league ball parks. The half was Braves Field in Boston. I went to Boston as a kid to see the Red Sox play in Fenway Park and when the game was over, I wanted to see Braves Field, which was nearby. I took a trolley over there but the place was closed. No matter. It was an old ball park and I walked all around it, peering through all the openings, getting some sense of what it was like in there, so I counted it as a half.

When I sent the column in, a young man called me at home and said he was a summer intern and they had given him my column to edit. He said: "It's a very fine column, Mr. Falls—I enjoyed it. But I have one question."

"What's that?"

"In this list of 37½ ball parks, would you like to include your own, Tiger Stadium?"

I blurted out: "38½." We both laughed. He was one smart kid.

I love old ball parks. I don't even like to call them stadiums. To me, Yankee Stadium is a ball park. So is Wrigley Field. And, certainly, Tiger Stadium, my home away from home for 45 years.

How this all started, I don't know. I think *The Sporting News*— where I wrote for 23 years—was responsible for much of it. We didn't have TV when I was growing up, so you had to use your imagination to envision what it was like when the Yankees (my team) were playing in Comiskey Park in Chicago or Sportsman's Park in St. Louis. You'd seen enough pictures in the papers to get some idea what those places were like—they even had some terrific clips in the movie "Pride of the Yankees." At least they tried to simulate these old fields and came pretty close. I even forgave them when they showed us, the Yankees, going around the American League and playing in Crosley Field, Cincinnati, which was in the National League.

This was during World War II and *The Sporting News* started carrying drawings of the old parks—a full half page, done by an artist name Gene Mack, who I found out later had done these drawings for the *Boston Globe* and were reproduced by *The Sporting News*. No matter. I could not wait for the next issue of *The Sporting News* because I wondered what ball park they would run. The paper would get to my neighborhood on a Wednesday but I found out there was a newsstand in Manhattan, in the heart of Times Square, that would get them on a Tuesday, so I took the subway over there every Tuesday afternoon and waited for the delivery truck to bring this great treasure.

To my disappointment, they did not run a ball park drawing every week, but I still went over to Times Square and held my breath when the truck would arrive. I would even help the guy take the papers off the truck because that way I was sure to get the first copy.

What I did with these drawings is put them on the floor and look at them when I was listening to the games on the radio. When Mel Allen would say Charley Keller just knocked one off the rightfield screen in Sportsman's Park, I could see it. Or I could watch them run up the terrace in leftfield of Crosley Field if I was listening to the Giants or Dodgers.

I dreamed of seeing all these ball parks one day.

The second summer I was in high school, I got a job as a messenger boy in mid-town Manhattan. We would sit in this office, 10 or 12 guys, waiting our turn to pick up something and deliver it. It was a good job because it got us out in the streets and we could enjoy the sights and sounds of the city.

The one job I wanted was the one to Philadelphia. Some company would send stuff down there and ask us to deliver it. When they picked other guys to make the trip, I would sulk. When was my turn? When could I take the train to Philadelphia? When could I go to Shibe Park and see the Phillies or the A's play?

One day, the boss said, "Falls! You're going to Philadelphia. Get the two o'clock train and have the stuff there by five o'clock. They're waiting for it."

They gave me the fare and I was on my way. We left out of Penn Station and I could feel my heart beating all the way. It was a 90-minute trip and I hustled over to Shibe Park from the North Philadelphia station—which, happily, was only a short distance away. Package? What package? I would deliver it later. The A's were playing the Tigers and I bought a ticket in the bleachers and sat in the lower leftfield deck, entranced by everything. Indian Bob Johnson was the leftfielder. He played right in front of me and it seemed as if I could reach out and touch him. I had his bubble gum card but here he was in the flesh. The game went 10 innings and I felt sad when it was over. I was hoping they'd play 17 innings.

But now, I'd better make that delivery. I was supposed to go to Independence Square and I took a bus and finally found it. The building was closed. It was after 6 p.m. A night watchman was there and I gave the package to him. I figured I'd lose my job but what the heck, I saw Eddie Mayo play second base for the Tigers and make a neat play into the hole.

As it turned out, I kept my job. Nothing was ever said about my late delivery but they never sent me to Philly again.

I used to go down there myself. I'd save up $5.25 for the train fare, round trip. While my buddies would go to the Polo Grounds, Yankee Stadium or Ebbets Field for the Sunday doubleheader, I'd take the train to Philadelphia. I'd sit in the grandstand, up high behind home plate, and try to get close to the press box because I might hear some of Byron Saam's broadcast. One day, Harry (The Hat) Walker got two triples and two bunt singles in a doubleheader, using that two-tone bat of his, and I thought I'd never seen a more artful hitter in my life. I told him this many years later in a meeting at Cooperstown; he didn't remember the two bunts or even the two triples but he sure liked hearing my words. We spoke for four hours straight.

I went to see the Yankees in Philadelphia and took pictures of the players—outfielders Russ Derry, Bud Metheny and Hershel Martin and pitcher Allen Gettel. These were the wartime Yankees but I loved those 5 x 8 photos. They were black and white and I carried them with me everywhere I went. I would take them out in class and study them instead of listening to the teacher. No wonder they had to give me bookkeeping and typing to graduate.

Shibe Park, with that massive wall in right, held a strong fascination for me. I'd read stories how Babe Ruth would hit the ball up on the roofs of the houses, and the ball could be seen bouncing through the rows of laundry.

Mel Ott, who used to be the greatest home run hitter in the National League—he had 511 when Ruth had 714—came to Detroit as a broadcaster in the late 1950s. Imagine, I got to know this great slugger. He was a terrific guy—quiet, friendly, almost withdrawn. I could not get over how his hands would shake when he went on the air. Mel Ott, nervous? He was barely able to light his cigarettes.

I used to kid him all the time: "511 homers, eh? How many did you hit in Shibe Park?"

I'd read somewhere that he had never connected in Shibe Park —just Baker Bowl, which was a bandbox. I never let him forget it, and he cussed me every time I brought it up. We became good friends, until he died in an auto accident in 1958.

I went to Washington to see a doubleheader in Griffith Stadium and could not take my eye off those trees which stood out behind the wall in dead center. That's where Ted Williams put one on opening day in 1946 in his first game after the war.

The big trip was to Boston. I'd always wanted to see the leftfield wall and, in 1947, I asked Jack Hand of The AP if he knew anyone on the Red Sox who could get me tickets to Fenway Park. He came up with them that quickly and I was on my way, saving enough dough to stay at the Statler Hilton Hotel in downtown Boston.

He got the tickets from Tom Dowd, who was the traveling secretary of the Red Sox. I'd never heard of him but got to know him later on and he is part of the history and tradition of baseball in Detroit. Dowd came into our ball park for a Sunday doubleheader and ate 18 double scoops of ice cream, two an inning, and this mark has never been challenged in all the ensuing years. Come to think of it, they don't serve ice cream in our press box anymore.

Dowd got me some terrific seats, for which I thanked him many times. They were in the front row, behind the Boston dugout, and I could look straight out at the "Green Monster."

On Sunday, the Red Sox played Connie Mack's Philadelphia A's and a strange thing happened. Boston was ahead 2-1 going into the bottom of the seventh when the Red Sox scored 14 runs—all of them off one pitcher, Carl Scheib, a young righthander. Even then, I knew something was wrong. You don't leave a pitcher in for 14 runs. The next day, Mr. Mack was quoted in the papers as saying he was "trying to teach the young man a lesson." What that lesson was, I never found out. Later in the season, Scheib started a game in Chicago and Mr. Mack left him for all nine runs in the first inning. I figured the young man was now the smartest pitcher in baseball.

I never knew Connie Mack, but I got very close to him. When the A's would come to Detroit, they would stay at the Ft. Shelby Hotel, just a half block from our AP office. On my dinner hour, I'd go over to the lobby and sit there and wait for him to show up. He did, on time, every night. He would sit there in that high-starched collar, tie and tightly fitting suit and read the evening paper. I would sit off to the side, pretending I was also reading, but I kept peering at him over the top of the paper.

George Kell told two great stories about Mr. Mack.

Kell played for him in the 1940s and said Mr. Mack would get up from his place on the bench along about the sixth inning, put on his suit jacket and walk out of the dugout. Not a word to anyone. He was just gone. In fact, they held the elevator just for him. Mr. Mack would get on, ride up to the front office and take a nap.

"Nobody said a word," Kell recalled. "It was all very natural. He'd leave and the third base coach, Al Simmons, or his son, Roy Mack, would simply take over and the game would go on."

Another time, Kell said Bobo Newsom was pitching for the A's and he was a blustery one. He was a rotund man and would huff and puff on and off the mound, his face turning beet red with the sweat pouring off his body.

The leftfielder (Roberto Estalella) made a bad play which let in some runs and Newsom got all over him when the inning was over. Mr. Mack saw it and bristled. But he didn't say a word to old Bobo until he got back to the clubhouse, and then, in his proper and genteel English, he let him have it.

Newsom listened for a moment, then said, "Aw, horseshit! Mr. Mack!"

Mr. Mack, shaking, trembling, summoning up all the courage at his command, replied, "And . . . and horsefeathers to you, Mr. Newsom!"

Shibe Park was the scene of another favorite story—this one involving Curt Gowdy, the broadcaster. He was working the Red Sox games when it started raining and play was suspended. He sent word up to the press box to see if Al Hirshberg, the celebrated writer, could come down to his broadcast booth and help him fill in the empty time.

Hirshberg showed up and Gowdy gave him a glowing introduction. Gowdy started interviewing him and as Hirshberg was into a long answer, Gowdy stood up, stretched, and walked out of the broadcast booth.

Hirshberg looked around, alarmed to be alone. But he knew the show had to go on. So he began rambling about a lot of topics, the state of the Red Sox, the pennant race—whatever came into his head.

Gowdy returned in about 10 minutes. Hirshberg was still talking away, getting more and more relaxed.

Gowdy sat down next to him. He said, "Al, what the hell are you doing. That's a dead mike. We've been off the air for 20 minutes . . ."

If I had to name my favorite ball park, it would be Ebbets Field in Brooklyn. No big deal. It was the favorite ball park of a lot of people.

Even though I was a Yankee fan, I saw more games in Ebbets Field than Yankee Stadium. Two reasons: 1. The games were more exciting. Something was always going on when the Dodgers were at home. The saying was, "Never a dull day with the Dodgers." It was true. 2. The bleacher seats had backs on them, just like the grandstand, with a roof over our heads, and we were close to the action. The bleachers were in the upper deck in centerfield and centerfield was only 376 feet from home plate.

And, of course, there was the wall. Even more marvelous than the wall in Boston. It was 40 feet high, half concrete, half screen, with advertising signs decorating the wall. Gem Razor. Botany ties. Bulova watches. And that Schaeffer beer sign on top of the scoreboard. On the bottom of the board was the Abe Stark sign: "Hit Sign, Win Suit." We all knew about it. Nobody, to our knowledge, ever won a vest, much less a suit. Dixie Walker and Carl Furillo, the Brooklyn rightfielders, wouldn't allow it.

I liked to play games with the New York writers.

I'd ask them: "What was at the bottom of the scoreboard in Ebbets Field?"

They would say, "Hit Sign, Win Suit." They would say it with disdain. Everyone knew about that sign.

"Whose sign was it? Who gave away these suits?"

Now, with a sneer: "Abe Stark, who else?" A clear victory for them.

"What was the address of his shop?"

Now, a vacant stare.

You waited. Five seconds. Ten seconds. Let them squirm.

Triumphantly: "1514 Pitkin Avenue." It was right there on the sign, but they never picked up on it.

A few years ago, when they started the all-women's team, the Colorado Silver Bullets, I went to Orlando to see them practice. The guy who ran the show was named Bob (no relation) Hope. He knew about Ebbets Field.

"You've got a great chance for a real promotional gimmick," I told him.

"What do you mean?" he asked.

"You'll have a scoreboard at your games, right?"

"Right."

"Just put a sign at the bottom of it."

"Saying what?"

"Hit Sign, Win Dress."

Little did I know but the Silver Bullets only played road games. Bob (nice guy) Hope laughed.

The best part of sitting in the bleachers was that you could see the balls sail over the screen into Bedford Ave. Guys would hang out in the gas station across the street and wait for the balls to come to them. Some of them had baseball gloves but it was a tough play because traffic was going both ways and you had to be careful of the cars, busses and trucks. Sometimes, the ball would roll through the filling station with half a dozen "fielders" in pursuit.

One day, to our utter delight, Babe Phelps—our beloved Blimp— got a hold of one and drove it out over the exit gate in right center. The ball bounced once and went crashing through the plate glass window of the car dealership across the way. You could see the glass shatter and you could hear it crashing to the sidewalk.

The Babe became an instant hero.

The next day there was a sign in the car dealership window: "Come on, Babe. Break our window. We love you."

I was standing at the batting cage in Yankee Stadium one day, watching the Tigers take batting practice, when a guy came up to me and said, "You're Joe Falls, right?"

"Guilty as charged," I said.

"I've been looking for you a long time," he said. "I've read all that stuff you've written about Ebbets Field and I want to tell you something."

"What's that?"

"I live in Brooklyn and I've got this kid," he said. "He's only 10 years old. He won't believe the Dodgers ever played in Brooklyn. All he knows is the Los Angeles Dodgers. No matter what I tell him, he won't believe me. He sees the Dodgers on TV and they're out in Los Angeles and that's it.

"One day I'm driving along Prospect Park Boulevard with my son and I say to myself: 'The hell with it. I'm going over to Bedford Avenue and show this little punk a thing or two.' I drive right up to the Ebbets Field Apartments and get out of the car. I take him with me, down this winding sidewalk, right to the front door. The sign says, 'Ebbets Field Apartments. Former Home of the Brooklyn Dodgers.'

"I say to him, 'See, now do you believe me that the Dodgers played here?' He looks at the sign, then looks at me, and says, 'Yeah, on what floor?'"

Another good thing about Ebbets Field was that it was so far from Manhattan the only way to get there—even for the players—was on the subway. It was too far and too expensive by taxi and nobody ever rented cars in those days.

If you played it right, you could wait for the visiting players to come out after the games and follow them to the Prospect Park Station and ride in the same train with them back to Manhattan. I never did this, though I did follow Dodger outfielder Pete Reiser and his wife one day as they were headed for the station. I hate to say it but I spent more time looking at his wife's legs than I did at Reiser.

I lucked out one day. I was coming home with a few of my friends, when who should be in the same car with us but Red Schoendienst, second baseman of the Cardinals. You couldn't miss him. He had a red complexion and his freckles had freckles.

I worked my way over to him in the crowded car. He was holding on to an overhead strap. I waited until the train pulled into a station when I knew we would all lose our balance and lurch forward a little bit. I let myself fall right into Schoendienst's back.

I had never talked to a ball player before, or asked for an autograph, but my day, and my life, were complete: I had actually touched one.

When the Tigers played the St. Louis Cardinals in the 1968 World Series, I went into Schoendienst's office before one of the games. He was the St. Louis manager. I told him what I had done on the subway that day, thinking he would find it humorous. Red was a nice man and tried to laugh but I don't think he thought it was so funny. In fact, I got the feeling he thought I was a little odd.

I have pictures of 17 old ball parks hanging in my den, plus a five-foot cardboard cutout of Ted Williams, my most cherished possession. I look straight at Ted from my computer and never tire of him in that white uniform with the blood-red "Red Sox" on his jersey, taking that famous swing and looking to the outfield where the ball is headed.

One of my all-time favorites was old Municipal Stadium in Kansas City. That's where they had that grass embankment behind the rightfield fence—a place where Charlie Finley, owner of the Kansas City A's, had technicolor sheep grazing on the grass. Yellow sheep. Blue sheep. Pink sheep. Green sheep. He even had a shepherd out there with him. One more private joke.

Finley liked private jokes.

Like the time Jerry Holtzman, the Chicago baseball writer, answered the doorbell of his home in Evanston, Illinois, on Christmas Eve and the delivery man had a large case for him with holes poked in the side. Holtzman signed for it, then brought it into his house. His kids—five, I believe—gathered around as he opened it. Out popped the cutest puppy dog in the Western Hemisphere. His children were besides themselves with joy.

That is, until a few months later, when the puppy started getting larger and larger, and Holtzman realized he had a St. Bernard on his hands. Finley's laughter could be heard all the way from his insurance office in downtown Chicago.

Municipal Stadium was where Finley set up his "Pennant Porch," no more than a ramshackled hut with a tin roof which accommodated a handful of fans. It was something like 297 feet from the plate and was supposed to be an answer to the short porch the Yankees had in rightfield in Yankee Stadium, also 297 feet away. The league eventually made Finley tear down his creation but he had his laugh, as well as plenty of publicity.

The "Pennant Porch" gave me an idea. I decided I would measure all the foul lines in the American League to see if they were accurate. I bought a steel tape from the hardware store and asked the players if they would help me. They were more than willing, especially the pitchers, since they wanted to find out where they were being fooled.

I decided to measure all the distances in Municipal Stadium and found every one of them off. The distances were shorter than the signs. Where it said 385, it was 365. I don't recall the exact numbers, but the A's had cheated everywhere in their ball park. Finley was trying to put some confidence into his pitchers.

He was furious when he read my story in *The Sporting News*.

He called George Toma, his groundskeeper, and asked him what the hell was going on. How did a sports writer get on the field to take all these measurements? He was about to fire Toma.

Poor George. He was a friend of mine from his days in the Detroit system, and he was lost for words. He told Finley, "I don't know how he got out there—I never saw him do it." And George didn't.

Finley kept him on because even he knew what a fine groundskeeper he had working for him—a man who, in later years, was commissioned by the National Football League to get their Super Bowl fields in shape.

Around the league we went with our steel tape measure. Half the foul lines were right, half were wrong. I was surprised about what we found out in Fenway Park in Boston. The books said it was 315 feet down the leftfield line but it looked a lot closer, probably because the wall loomed so high. They did not have a sign down there but it came out to exactly 315 feet.

The big expose took place in Yankee Stadium.

You may recall that 297 marker in right—the one that created so much controversy over the years. Critics said it was a cinch shot for Babe Ruth and helped him to his awesome home run records. When we measured that one, the ground crew tried to throw me off the field. They were screaming all over the place. But the players wouldn't let them get near me. They formed a circle around me, threatening anyone who tried to break us up, and we measured this one four times—twice out and twice back and guess what? That fabled 297 foot sign should have read 292—so it was easier than anyone thought for the great Bambino.

I was in Candlestick Park on the day of the great rumble in the 1989 World Series between the San Francisco Giants and Oakland A's. I had just taken my seat in the auxiliary press box high in the upper deck and wasn't feeling too comfortable about it. I have a distinct case of vertigo (which goes nicely with my claustrophobia) and I could see nothing but sky as I looked around. No houses. No building. No trees. No nothing. Just sky.

That's when everything started shaking.

I thought it was the usual pre-game fly-over by some jets and looked up to see the planes. I didn't see any planes. I looked down at the seats along the first base line into rightfield and everyone seemed to be holding onto something.

The next thing I knew, I had jumped out of my seat and wound up on all fours on the concrete landing behind my row. I was looking directly into the face of a writer from Houston whom I didn't know. He was also down on all fours. He said, "I think we're having an earthquake."

I could envision the stands collapsing and everyone in the upper deck falling into the people in the lower deck. I had nothing to hold onto, so I just rocked back and forth as the concrete under me rocked back and forth.

Then it stopped. It lasted only 15 seconds but seemed much longer. More like 15 hours. I looked out at the people in the centerfield stands and I could hear them cheering. I thought, "Are they nuts? Cheering an earthquake?"

Cooler minds told me later that they were cheering the fact that the earthquake was over and we had all survived.

I knew one thing: I was getting out of there as quickly as possible. I picked up my things and bolted for the exit gate. I started down the ramps with about a dozen other people. Don't ask me to explain this, but when we got to the gate, we all stopped to get our hands stamped so we could get back in.

I once saw lightning hit the field at Memorial Stadium in Baltimore. The Tigers were playing a Saturday afternoon game against the Orioles when the rains fell and play was suspended. They'd covered the field with a tarp when a flash of lightning struck just behind shortstop, creating a giant puff of smoke and sending a crashing noise throughout the stadium.

When the rains stopped, Willie Tasby refused to come out of the Baltimore dugout and they had to send somebody in to play centerfield for him.

In Detroit, I've seen hail as large as—well, how did they ever measure hail before we had golf balls? Once, it rained so much that the corridor back to the clubhouse filled with four feet of water and the players had to go through the stands to get to the clubhouse. Ah, Detroit: Where the sign on the visitors' dressing room used to say: "Visitors' Dressing Room—No Visitors Allowed."

We've felt two earthquakes in Tiger Stadium, tremors from as far away as Indiana and Missouri. Both times the press box swayed back and forth, though the players on the field felt nothing.

One winter's night in 1974, the press box caught fire and burned up. They summoned Jim Campbell, the general manager who lived downtown, and he quickly drove out to the ball park. He stood in the outfield with some firemen and looked up at the blaze.

Campbell was shaking his head.

"Too bad, Jim," one of the fire fighters said.

"Yeah," said Campbell. "Too bad the press box was empty."

I always dreamed of catching a foul ball when I was kid but they always seemed to fall into other people's hands. So, I would beat the game. I got my baseball mitt and went to the Polo Grounds early, even before they opened the gates, and I would stand in the upper rightfield deck and catch one. After all, it was only 257 feet down the line and they were knocking them up there all through batting practice.

When I got there, there were four or five other guys waiting— all with baseball gloves. Not such a good idea, Joe. But I stayed and took my chances.

Johnny Rucker of the Giants was in the cage and he ripped one down the line. It was coming right at me. I got ready. I couldn't believe how fast it was flying and when it got to me, I had all I could do to duck. It went sailing over my head. The ball hit the back of an exit ramp and bounced back and hit me in the back of the neck, nearly knocking me over. It rolled away and one of the other guys merely bent over and picked it up, smiling at me as he did.

Once, in Griffith Stadium in Washington, somebody hit a foul ball into a front row box just to the right of the screen. Two men dove for it. They wrestled on the ground, rolling around on the dirty concrete. One guy, with a torn shirt and his glasses knocked sideways, came up with it and held it aloft for all to see. He was covered with dirt.

He gave the ball to a small boy, presumably his son, and the boy took one look at it and tossed it back on the field.

The golden moment finally arrived at the Polo Grounds. It was during the war and I went to the game with my brother, Ed, who was in the Army. He was wearing his uniform and these were the days when the ball clubs asked the fans to throw the balls back onto the field so they could be sent to the various camps so the servicemen could play their games.

A good idea, but the public being the public was suspicious and started tossing the balls to the servicemen in the stands. A friend of mine had also gone to the game with us, getting there early to hold the seats, and he caught a foul ball when batting practice started. Then, during the game, the fans threw two more balls to my brother, who waved to them, and now we had three baseballs in one day.

I felt like a king.

As you know, baseballs can do a lot of damage. Back in the 50s, they used to serve drinks in the press box at Briggs Stadium. In fact, they had a bar in the back of the press box in Briggs Stadium. Anything you wanted—scotch, bourbon, rye. Name it and John the bartender would fix it.

One day, Lloyd Northhard, Jr., of the UPI had a tall one at his side when a ball came screaming into the press box. It hit the top of the glass and broke the glass off smoothly. The top half of it was gone—shattered—but not a drop of the drink was spilled.

On opening day in 1955, the press box was crowded with writers, as it always was on opening day. Some guys came in for only one game a year. This was the day. I was sitting next to H.G. Salsinger, the longtime sports editor of *The Detroit News*. He was on the job for 50 years and was the man who had the ear of Frank Navin, the old owner, talking him into getting catcher Mickey Cochrane from the Philadelphia A's— a move that led to two pennants and a World Series in the 1930s.

Sal was a legend, almost a deity. He never came around much since he was in his 70s but commanded complete respect when he did show up. He knew them all, back to Ty Cobb, Harry Heilmann and Sam Crawford. The rest of us knew Al Aber, Jack Dittmer and Jim Delsing.

The newly formed Baltimore Orioles (formerly the St. Louis Browns) were playing their first game in the American League. Steve Gromek was pitching for the Tigers, and now he was at the plate.

Gromek fouled one back, high into the press box. Lyall Smith, sports editor of *The Detroit Free Press*, cried, "LOOK OUT!"

With that, Mr. Salsinger looked up from his typewriter and the ball crashed into his face. It hit him under his eye and sent him sprawling back to the wall behind us. I scrambled to the floor to help him but the blood was spurting from his face as if propelled by a pump. It was shooting back over to where he was sitting, flying out of the press box and down to the stands below. I held my hand in front of his face to stop the flow and got blood all over my arm.

They took Sal away in an ambulance. He lost the sight of his eye and never returned to the ball park.

This is what I thought about that day in Lakeland when a ball smashed into me when I wasn't looking.

The Tigers were playing an exhibition game with the Philadelphia Phillies and by now we no longer were writing with typewriters. We were using computers, with their little lighted screens, which was fine, except the one I had wasn't lighted. It was a Tandy 200 and worked on the theory of reflected light. You could see the screen very well if there was light behind you. In a press box, the light comes in, and so I had trouble seeing the screen.

What I would do is turn around, so the light was behind me, and write on a table in the back of the press box. Even though I could not follow the game, I could get my work done.

Someone on the Phillies—I've forgotten his name—sent a whistler back into the press box. I never saw it or heard it. I only felt it. It slammed into the middle of my back, between the shoulder blades, and it felt as if somebody had hit me with a sledgehammer. I lost my breath, nearly fell off the chair, and remembered the story I had read in the papers that morning: A father coaching third base in a Little League game was hit in the chest by a line drive. He seemed OK but dropped dead a half hour later.

As the guys gathered around me to see if I was OK, I told them I was fine and went straight to the men's room and locked the door. I had a lot of class in those days. I decided if I was going to die in a half hour, I would die with dignity by myself. How they would ever get the bathroom door open, I didn't know. I didn't even think about it. But I sat on the potty with my pants pulled up for a full 30 minutes before I emerged again.

Tom Gage, our baseball writer at the *News*, kept knocking on the door asking if I was all right. I kept telling him I was OK. Later on, I told everyone that Tom really wanted my job and when the ball came flying into the press box as I was writing, he cried, "Look out."

Chapter 5:
Fear of Flying (and Drinking)

Gloria Bell is the wife of Buddy Bell, manager of the Tigers, and she had it exactly right: "When Buddy started playing in the major leagues, it seemed so glamorous, living in those fine hotels, going to the movies and out to dinner. Now we both know it's not much fun being away from home. It can be a burden on everyone."

Travel.

If you're in this business of sports, you can't live without it and it is hard to live with it. Almost everyone tires of it, except Ernie Harwell. The celebrated broadcaster has been doing it for more than 50 years and seems to relish banging around the country with a ball club. He can tell you the name of every fine restaurant in the American League, even what's on the menu. He knows all the people in his job and they know him. He has had a wonderful life.

Flying used to be fun. A great adventure. The planes were new and the stewardesses were pretty. That was one of the requisites for getting the job—maybe the main one. You had to be attractive. Imagine them trying to do that these days? It was easy getting in and out of airports. Park your car in the partially filled lots, walk through the near empty terminals and get on the planes. No trouble. No hassle. No people. If you traveled with the Tigers, the bus would take you right to plane side, right to the bottom of the steps. You simply left your air-conditioned hotel, rode on the air-conditioned bus and got on the air-conditioned plane. These were charters, reserved for the team, and as you walked down the aisle, they had all sorts of goodies waiting for you—cookies, candy, fruit, pop, beer and nuts...merely a preview of what was to come. The only real problem was that all the airlines served steak on every flight. I could see the chefs in the kitchen talking to each other: "What do ball players like to eat?" "Baseball players like to eat steak." It got so bad Ernie and I never ate the main meal. The aroma alone was repelling. Ernie called it "Steak a la Sog." The players didn't care. They'd devour them as quickly as they were served. Gus Zernial could put away four or five with no trouble. I used to bring deli sandwiches on the plane when we were leaving from Detroit. Once, coming out of Boston, somebody made a grievous mistake and served franks and beans. I cheered out loud.

The planes left on time and arrived on time. The only time I didn't appreciate this was when we were flying into Charleston, West Virginia, for an exhibition game against the Minnesota Twins. Both teams were coming out of Florida at the end of spring training and were going to play a weekend series in Charleston. As we approached the airport, our plane dove to the left, almost straight down, and we came in under full throttle. It seemed the Twins' plane was about to land at the same time. Bud Jordan, our pilot, ducked in under them and got in first. He proudly announced over the intercom: "Nobody beats the Detroit Tigers in anything."

We were going from Seattle to Oakland, flying over the mountains. The guys said, "Hey, look, there's Mt. St. Helen's down there." As I looked out the window—a mistake—the plane dipped sharply to the left and started dropping. The pilot knew the Tigers were aboard and wanted to give them a good look at the smoldering volcano. He flew all around it while I flew back to my seat and closed my eyes.

Today, flying can be a chore. If you fly, you know what I mean. If you don't fly, just stay home and watch it all on TV.

I was on the first plane trip the Tigers ever took. It was out of spring training in 1956. They were going from Lakeland to Houston for a weekend series against the Yankees. It was a long train trip and the players asked if they could go by air. Spike Briggs was owner of the team, a man who understood his players. He granted them permission but under one condition: the plane could not go out over the Gulf of Mexico. If anything was going to happen, Briggs wanted them to be able to land. No going down in the drink.

They loaded up a two-engine DC-3, a prop plane, and away we went. Or so we hoped. Nobody knew much about flying and they packed the plane with everything—bats, balls, gloves, equipment and trunks. They took along 28 players instead of the usual 25. They were allowed to carry three extra players for the first few weeks of the season. They also had a full complement of writers and club officials. The plane was so heavy that when it started down the runway at old Drain Field in Lakeland, it could not lift off the ground and we ran out of runway.

I was sitting in a window seat and could see what was happening. Here we were in a field, bouncing along the ground, unable to get airborne. Jack Homel, the trainer, was sitting across the aisle. He took one look at me and started laughing.

"Your biggest story," he said, "and you'll never get to write it."

The plane slowly lifted and strained to get into the sky. Ever since that day, I have hated flying, which is too bad because all I've done in my job is fly.

I once came back from a pro football game in Washington and the plane bounced all over the place. I thought we were going to die. I always think we're going to die.

When I got home, I told my wife: "That's it—no more flying. I'm done. If they don't play it here, I ain't going."

She said: "Take a look at today's paper. They've got a story in there about 'Fear of Flying.' One of our schools is giving lessons. Maybe you ought to call them up."

I was scheduled to fly to Europe later that week on assignment and went to the phone the next morning.

A lady answered. I did not tell her who I was but said I was having a problem flying.

"I have to go to Europe in a few more days and I'm very nervous about it. When is your first lesson?" This was on a Monday morning.

She said, "Our first lesson this week is on Wednesday."

"How many lessons can I take before I leave on Friday?"

"Just one," she said.

I held my hand over the phone and told my wife: "I can take only one lesson before Friday."

My wife said, "Why don't you ask them if you can take a crash course?"

I've had my share of close calls. While landing in San Francisco with the Detroit Lions, a fire broke out on one of the engines. Joe Schmidt, the captain and middle linebacker, looked out the window and said, "It looks like we're going to burn up." Just what I needed to hear.

I looked out the window and saw a fire blazing in the engine and blowing black smoke over the wing. Luckily, we were within a few minutes of landing (enough time for 10 Our Fathers and 10 Hail Marys). We came down very easily. When we got off, I looked at the plane. The wing and side of the plane were burned black.

It was an American Airlines plane and Walter Boyd, the rep who flew with us, said, "Aw, it's nothing. Just a stack fire."

Just a stack fire. That made me feel a lot better.

Another time we were landing in Minneapolis and they told us to remove all sharp objects from our pockets, take off our shoes, put a pillow in front of our faces and lean forward in our seats. It seems the landing gear light would not come on and they didn't know if the wheels were locked into place.

I looked out the window and could see a line of fire trucks, ambulances and police cars waiting for us. We came down smoothly as these vehicles raced down the runway behind us.

Years later, I thought about that incident. The sharp objects, I could understand. Even the pillows and leaning forward. But taking off our shoes? What was that all about? How could that make it safer? If we had to run away from the plane, I didn't want to do it in my stocking feet.

Minneapolis was the scene of our closest call. We were making a tour of the Big Ten football camps on the annual Skywriter's Tour, and as our DC-3 was taking off, I was in the back putting some of the luggage away. We had to put the bags on and take them off and we took turns seeing all was in place. It was my turn.

We could not have been up a couple of thousand feet when the plane suddenly plunged downward, as if it had lost all its power. I was thrown to the floor. Pressed against the floor was more like it. You'd think if the plane was going down, you would go up toward the ceiling. Not this time. I was pinned to the floor as the plane kept falling. I managed to pull myself up and looked out the window. I could see trees—a forest of them—coming up at us and thought this was it. The plane leveled off and started climbing, missing those trees by a small margin. Later we learned we had missed a mid-air collision with a United Airlines jet that was taking off. This was my last Skywriter's trip.

One Sunday the Tigers played a doubleheader in Kansas City. The games went into darkness and when they were over, they told us to hurry up—a storm was coming and they wanted to get to the airport before it hit.

We must have flown right into it—a heavy hailstorm—because our Continental plane heaved over on its side shortly after takeoff, and we were flying sideways. All the stuff in the bins on the right side of the cabin flew over to the left side. It lasted only a few second before we straightened out, but I thought we were going to die.

"No problem," said pitcher Hank Aguirre. "No problem at all." His shirt and his jacket were soaked with sweat.

Willie Horton, the outfielder, hated to fly. So, naturally, the players kept locking him in the bathroom by piling all the bags in front of the door.

Two players—who shall go unnamed—liked to play tricks on the stewardesses.

They would bring along a can of Dinty Moore beef stew and open it after we were airborne. One of them would pretend he was sick and took a barf bag and acted as if he was throwing up into the bag. He had put some of the beef stew into the bag.

The other player would call for the stewardess and she would rush to the player's aid. The player would hand her the bag but before she could take it away, he would say, "One minute, please. There's a good piece in there." He would reach into the bag and take a piece of the beef and start chewing on it. How can I describe the look on the stewardess' face?

One night we were flying somewhere when they put the seat belt sign on and announced we were headed into some turbulence. It got very bumpy. Pitcher Dan Petry got up from his seat and went up the aisle and sat next to Ernie Harwell, who was calmly reading a book.

If you know Ernie at all, he is one of the most devout Christians in baseball, a man who usually heads up the Sunday services for the players in the clubhouse.

Later, I asked Petry: "Why'd you go up there and sit with Ernie?"

He said: "If he was going anywhere, I wanted to go with him."

George Cantor, who was our baseball writer at *The Detroit Free Press*, had a simple philosophy about flying. He never got scared. He figured if Al Kaline was on the plane, nothing bad could happen. He said, "God would not let anything happen to Al Kaline."

We were playing in Kansas City and a tornado alarm sounded. The skies darkened and a heavy rain started falling. Some tar paper from the roof blew onto the field and Cantor got up from his seat in the press box and went into the broadcast booth and asked George Kell if he could sit next to him.

"Why'd you do that?" I asked later on.

George replied, "As far as I know, nobody has ever been killed by a tornado while telecasting a baseball game from Kansas City."

George took my place as baseball writer at the *Free Press* in 1965. That's when I moved up to columnist. He was, and is, a fussy one, very involved in creature comforts. His creature comforts.

When we went to St. Louis for the start of the 1968 World Series, they got the hotel rooms mixed up and George had to share a room with photographer Dick Tripp. Not only that, they had to share the same bed.

When George awoke in the morning, he was screaming. "Never again!" he bellowed. "Never will I sleep with anyone ever again! I was up all night. I couldn't sleep a wink. I feel terrible."

Yes, George.

During the night, a burglar made his way into their room and took their money and jewelry. In fact, he nailed everyone on the floor except pitching coach Willis Hudlin, who put his money under a Bible on the dresser.

I have no idea why Kansas City has played such a prominent part in my travel troubles. Maybe it's tornado country. Or maybe it's just my imagination.

I could never figure out why, when we were flying out of Kansas City, the plane would sit at the end of the runway and shake before we started our takeoff. It was not until years later that I found out the pilot was building up power, with the brakes locked, so he could become airborne as quickly as possible. The runway pointed straight toward downtown Kansas City and he had to get up as fast as he could in order to clear the tall buildings.

Another time we were flying to Kansas City on a four-engine plane when one of the engines conked out. The pilot told us he had to "feather" it because it was giving him some trouble. No problem, though, he said. He would just detour to Chicago and everything would be okey-dokey. That's what he said. Okey-dokey.

As I walked down the aisle, I could feel my feet pressing into the floor. Okey-dokey, my butt.

When we landed, I knew I would have to call my office and tell them what happened. I knew how my office would react. I was working for *The Detroit Times,* a Hearst paper, and while I cannot say we delved into yellow journalism, we were known to color things up a bit. We were last in the market of three newspapers and did little things to get the public's attention.

I talked to Ed Hayes, my boss. I told him what had happened and said everything was all right and we were getting another plane to take us to Kansas City. I hung up with a grave feeling of apprehension.

The next day, *The Detroit Times* carried a story on page one with an eight-column headline: "Tiger Plane Forced Down." Guess whose byline was on the story.

John McHale, Sr., was running the Tigers in those days. Ed Hayes called him up to get his reaction to the story. McHale was furious.

He said he was going to demand an investigation into the incident. He thought it was a two-engine plane, while Hayes was talking about a four-engine plane. McHale's quotes were pretty strong and resulted in another page-one story the next day.

One guy who hated flying even more than I did was third baseman Ray Boone. When the weekend series in Kansas City was over and we were walking out to the plane, he stopped and took a piece of paper from his pocket. I was walking with him and could see a lot of numbers written on the paper. Boone looked at the paper, then at the airplane. He checked the numbers and realized it was the same plane that had lost an engine a few days earlier.

"See you guys later," said Boone, turning around and walking away. He took the train back to Detroit.

Ah, train travel.

I came in late on this end of the business. We've all heard the stories of how wonderful train travel was in the old days—how teams would command entire Pullman cars and dining cars and how they'd sit up into the night playing cards, drinking, smoking cigars and talking baseball (or, I guess, girls).

Rick Ferrell, the old catcher, told of his first train trip in the majors. It was back in 1929 with the St. Louis Browns. The team was going to New York and Rick was a raw rookie and didn't want to do the wrong things.

"I decided I would follow one of the veteran players and do just what he did," Ferrell recalled. "I picked out Lu Blue, the first baseman. He'd been around a long time. When he got off the train at Grand Central, I got off the train. When he picked up his bag on the platform, I picked up my bag. When he started walking away, I followed him.

"He went up the stairs, crossed the station and went down another flight of stairs. I was right behind him. Finally, he turned around and said, 'Where are you going?'

"I told him, 'I'm following you to the hotel.'

"'That's fine,' he said, 'but I'm going to my home in New Rochelle.'"

My first train trip with the Tigers was in 1957. We were going to New York to start an eastern trip and were leaving out of Michigan Central depot at about seven o'clock at night.

Reno Bertoia, a rookie third baseman, was standing on the platform and looking uneasy. He was from across the river in Windsor and was a nice guy and so I started talking to him.

"What's the matter, Reno? You look worried."

"Aw, it's nothing," he said.

"Come on, something is bothering you."

He held up a brown bag. "It's just this," he said. "Meatball sandwiches. My mother didn't think they'd feed me properly, so she made me these meatball sandwiches."

Before I could say anything, Harvey Kuenn and Billy Hoeft, two vets, walked up and said, "Did somebody say meatball sandwiches?"

Reno's face started getting red.

"We will be glad to dispose of them for you," said Kuenn, reaching for the bag. They left laughing. Reno seemed relieved.

Later that night, I had my first experience of riding with a major league team. When dinner was over, Mel Ott, the great National League slugger who was working on the Tigers' radio broadcasts, asked some of the guys if they'd like to come by his compartment for a few drinks. He invited me, even though I didn't drink.

For the next few hours, I was entranced by what I heard. Master Melvin regaled us with stories of his life in the National League when he was a player, then manager, of the New York Giants. He told us of the day he walked Bill Nicholson of the Chicago Cubs with the bases loaded. Nicholson, Big Swish, had hit four home runs in a doubleheader and Ott was determined he would not beat them with a fifth homer. The strategy worked and the Giants got an even split for the day. Ott told us of the mind games he played with Leo Durocher when Leo was managing the Brooklyn Dodgers. He told us of the games against those great St. Louis Cardinal teams. It was after two o'clock in the morning and I was so stimulated, I couldn't sleep.

We got to Grand Central just before eight o'clock in the morning and I went to the phone and woke my wife up back in Detroit.

"Honey, you'll never believe what happened on the train last night."

I wasn't even tired. I was so thrilled at hearing all these wonderful stories that I couldn't get all my words out quickly enough.

Later in the trip, we took the train from Baltimore to Boston and once again Ott invited a few of us to his compartment for a few drinks and little more baseball talk. I took a seat in the corner and made myself comfortable and waited in wonder until the words would spill out of this man.

One hour later, I excused myself, never feeling more deflated in my life.

Ott told the same stories, in the same words—how he walked Nicholson, how he jousted with Durocher, how he went up against those great teams in St. Louis. I was crushed. I never mentioned this to my wife. I liked Mel too much. He was really a neat guy.

Our traveling secretary was a man named Frank Contway. He was a friend of owner Spike Briggs, which is why he got the job. He worked in Briggs' auto dealership in Lake Wales, Florida, but now he was shepherding his team around the country.

Contway liked to drink. One night we went to Tampa for dinner and he had a little too much. He drove back to Lakeland, going faster and faster on the darkened two-lane road, until the police started chasing us just outside of Lakeland. I was hunched in the back seat, trying to disappear.

Contway zoomed up to a Catholic church and ran inside. The cops went in after him and pulled him out. He must have thought nobody ever gets arrested while claiming sanctuary.

One time in New York, trainer Jack Homel was sound asleep when there was a knocking on his door. He tried to pay no attention to it but the knocking grew louder and stronger.

"One minute! One minute!" he said, pulling himself out of bed. It was in the middle of the night and he was stark naked.

Homel opened the door on the crack and saw that it was Contway —in his usual condition.

"Come on, open up, Buddy! Let's have a little touch."

Homel said, "Go to bed! You're out of it!"

Contway saw Homel's condition—not a stitch of clothing—and grabbed him by the wrist and pulled him into the hallway.

Click!

The door snapped shut behind them, locked tightly.

Contway started laughing and walked away.

"Come back here!" Homel cried. "You can't leave me like this."

Contway was gone, singing a merry little tune.

Ding!

It was the sound of the elevator stopping on the floor. Homel panicked and raced down the hall away and around the corner. He slipped into a small utility room, where the brooms and pails were put away for the night. He saw a small washcloth draped over the sink. He held it front of him.

A guy walked by. Homel opened the door on the crack and said, "Pssssst!" That's all he could get out. The guy took one look at him, holding a washcloth in front of his naked body, and took off down the hallway. It was not until the third guest came by that Homel got any help.

I didn't care who drank or who did what. I felt it was none of my business. If the ball club wanted to take any action, then it was my business and I'd go for the story. Kuenn was the big drinker on the team. One Saturday night I went to the movies in New York and decided to walk back to the hotel. It was near midnight and Lexington Ave. was pretty crowded; and I felt it would be safe to walk from 58th street to 42nd street.

When I was halfway there, I was walking past a bar when some guy came lurching out of the door. It was Kuenn. I stepped back into the shadows so he wouldn't see me. I liked Harvey—he was a good guy—and didn't want to embarrass him.

There was a taxi parked at the curb and as he reached for the handle on the back door, the cab pulled away, spinning him around. He went wobbling back into the bar.

"Oh, my," I said to myself. The Tigers had a doubleheader with the Yankees the next day. I said nothing to anyone about what I had seen.

The Tigers won both games and Al Kaline and Kuenn got 15 hits in the doubleheader.

Another who liked his good times was first baseman Norm Cash. He could skip sleep and also get the job done.

Once, in Kansas City, Cash was rooming with catcher Jim Price. He came in late on a Saturday night in a very unsettled condition. The Tigers had a doubleheader the next day and Price was worried about his roommate.

Cash owned an expensive watch and decided it was time to toss it out the window. The watch landed in the middle of the street. Price looked out the window and saw it down there. He quickly left the room wearing a minimum of clothes and went outside to retrieve the watch before anyone else could get to it.

The police saw him and took him to headquarters and wanted to book him for indecent exposure. When Price convinced them who he was and what had happened, they let him go. When he got back to the room, Cash was sound asleep, with his clothes on. The next day, Cash got nine hits in the doubleheader.

The best part of travel is you get a chance to spend time with your buddies in the business. My best friends worked for *The Toledo Blade*.

Don Wolfe, sports editor of *The Blade*, was a bear-like man who was given to great cheer. He found humor in everything. At his retirement party, he said the biggest change in journalism in his time were how many women got into the business. He said, "As I was telling my Avon Man this morning..."

Don didn't know a lot about sports but he knew a lot about people.

When I started my first column, he said, "You'll never get the first one written."

"Thank you, Don."

"No, I mean it. I know you. You'll never be able to write your first column. I suggest you start with the word 'The' and go on from there."

I thought he was nuts.

When I sat down to write, he was right. My mind was a blank. I couldn't get the first word down on my paper. So, I typed the word "The." It did not exactly flow after that, but at least I had a start.

He said, "What are you going to call your column?"

"I don't know."

"Why don't you call it 'Red Smith by Joe Falls.' There is only one other like it in the country and maybe nobody will notice. Or you could call it, 'Over the Barrel by Joe Falls' or 'Over the Falls by Joe Barrel.'"

Don is gone now and I know exactly how I will end my last column.

The...

End.

The Tigers had a catcher named J.W. Porter. Nice kid. Friendly. Freckle-faced. We all liked him because he was a colorful character. He'd go into greasy spoons after the games and order "24 over light." They'd look at him. He wanted 24 eggs over light. They never believed him, not even when he ate all the eggs.

When we were in New York, Porter was served with papers in a paternity suit. A woman in Buffalo charged him with fathering her baby. We went to court that day but missed the story when Porter scrambled down the back stairs of the courthouse.

We asked manager Bucky Harris for his comment at the game that night and Harris replied: "Does anyone really care where Porter puts his... "

Don Wolfe cared. He found out that Porter liked to write poetry. When we got to Cleveland, he interviewed him for a column.

Wolfe separated each section of the column with a little limerick about Porter.

While the other players are down in the lobby,
Porter's in his room practicing his hobby.

Don took his eight-year-old son to Cleveland for a weekend series with the Indians. Normally, he drove. This time he took the train so his son could have all the experiences of traveling. Don did everything possible with the boy over the three-day trip. He took him to the games, introduced him to the players and let him get autographs. He took him to the finest restaurants, to a movie, to the zoo—even a boat trip. On the way home on the train, he said to his son: "What impressed you most about this weekend?"

The boy thought for a moment and said, "You know our bathroom in the hotel?"

"Yes," said Don.

"How do they get the toilet paper to go into the wall?" the boy asked.

Eddie Jones of the *Toledo Blade* was next. He was the softie of all softies. He liked to drink, and when he drank, he began crying. He felt bad for the poor people of the world. At Christmas, his office would have to hold back his paycheck and deliver it personally to his wife, Jane. Eddie usually cashed it and went around town giving money to the indigent.

I loved this man because of his compassion for others. Whenever I started getting impressed with myself, he'd cut me down. No one ever taught me more about the dangers of self-aggrandizement.

We covered the Baltimore Colts-New York Giants' championship game for the NFL title in New York in 1958. It was a memorable day, one that football fans still talk about. When Steve Myhra kicked that field goal to force overtime, I slammed my fist on the desk in delight. I wanted the Colts to win because Johnny Unitas was the best quarterback I had ever seen.

As we were walking up the ramp to the press box, Eddie stopped and said, "Wait a minute, I've got to catch my breath."

We stood there for a few minutes, then continued on. When the game ended, Eddie wrote his column, a story of the game and some notes. We were staying together at a hotel in mid-town Manhattan and I thought he deserved something nice so I ordered up a full meal from room service. Eddie just picked at it and we did not know, until he got back to Toledo the next day, that he had suffered a heart attack walking up that ramp. He later died of another heart attack.

Tom Loomis took over Jones' column. He, too, loved Eddie. Tom was my best friend, along with Doug Mintline of the *Flint Journal*, and if you've never heard of them, that's OK. They never did anything to draw attention to themselves. They were simply good men, old-fashioned journalists who did their jobs well.

Like so many others, Tom liked to drink. We went to The Masters one year when they announced, at mid-afternoon, that they had a special treat in the press hut.

It was something new: Michelob beer on tap. Come one, come all. Ice cold. All you can drink. Free of charge.

I knew this could be a problem. I finished my work before Tom and told him I'd meet him back at the hotel for dinner.

At 4 a.m. the phone rang in my room. It was the Augusta police. They were holding a Mr. Tom Loomis of the *Toledo Blade* and could I come down and pick him up. By now, Tom was sober and couldn't understand what all the fuss was about.

I started drinking when I was a copy boy with The AP in New York but I didn't get very far with it. Maybe five drinks. I was 18. Spike Claassen, the assistant sports editor, asked if I'd like to go to the annual Basketball Writer's Association dinner at Toots Shore. Would I? I wore my best clothes and we went over there, just across the street, after work at five o'clock.

The place was jammed. Guys everywhere. Drinking. Smoking. Talking. Laughing. I stopped at the door, trying to assimilate this scene. Spike went ahead and started shaking hands with a lot of people I didn't know. Heck, I didn't know anyone.

A waiter came up to me. He was holding a tray.

"Would you care for a martini, sir?"

Why not? I had to do something to look like I belonged. I took a drink and downed it.

Another waiter came by.

"Would you like a Manhattan, sir?"

Sure. I took it and downed that one, too.

It took only 30 minutes for the room to start turning. I was still standing near the door, afraid to go any further, and everything was going around and around.

I knew I had to leave. I did not want to embarrass my boss. I turned and walked out the door. I knew where I was—on 50th street, just off Fifth Avenue. I knew I had to get home. I had to get one of those double decker busses to take me to Queens.

I waited on the corner and when I saw my bus, I got on, shakily, and decided it would be best if I went upstairs. Fewer people could see me up there.

I sat in the front row and when the bus pulled away, I fell over on the side and went to sleep.

I awoke at 1 a.m. and thought I had gone to hell. It was very dark. I couldn't see a thing. I sat up and looked around. I had no idea where I was or what had happened.

I sat there for several minutes trying to collect myself. I finally realized where I was. I was in the front seat of a double deck bus and there were other busses parked all around me. I had slept through the entire trip—over the Queensboro Bridge, through my neighborhood out to somewhere where they had parked the bus in a garage for the night. I was in Jackson Heights, about five or six miles from home.

I gathered myself and walked down the stairs at the back of the bus. I could see a small light off in a distance. It was the night watchman's office. I went over and talked to him and figured I may as well be honest about it. I told him what I had done. He smiled and said I should go out the door, turn left, and walk up to the subway station. That would take me home.

My mother was up waiting for me.

When I walked into the living room, she said, "Are you all right?"

"I'm all right."

"You'd better get to bed."

She never mentioned the incident again. She was a great mother.

My other major drinking episode was when I went to the West Coast with the Lions for their 1957 playoff game with the San Francisco 49ers. That was the one where the Lions overcame a 27-7 deficit to beat the 49ers and get into the NFL title game.

We stayed at Ricky's Motel in Palo Alto and if you've never been to heaven, Ricky's would do as a proper substitute. Talk about sumptuous. They had palatial gardens, with marble statues, wonderful food—bands that played at lunch and dinner—and swings in every room.

Yes, swings.

You could sit on them and swing back and forth all day long if you wished.

The Lions knew I was a tee-totaler and so, at breakfast, coach George Wilson, who had a bit of the rascal in him, talked me into trying a screwdriver.

I had never even heard of a screwdriver.

"You'll like it," he said. "Lots of orange juice. Very healthy for you."

I tried one, then two, then three and they all left to go to practice. When they returned for lunch, I was on the stage singing with the band. They urged me on.

I also missed the afternoon practice. I remained in my room, swinging on the swing.

Bud Erickson was the publicity man and he knew I was about to get into trouble. I had to get a story back to my paper. Bud rounded up the other writers and they came to my room.

I was swinging and singing away.

Erickson said, "OK, guys . . . we take turns. Each one writes a paragraph." Doc Greene of *The Detroit News* was first, followed by Bob Latshaw of *The Free Press,* then some outstate writers. Even Bud took a turn.

They all pounded out their paragraph and came back a few more times for another shot at it. Obviously, a competition soon set in—who could write the best paragraph?

Who cared? Swing and sing, swing and sing.

Bud drove me down to the Western Union office and filed the story to my paper, *The Detroit Times.* I was stretched out on the back seat, singing as loudly as I could.

The next day, my boss, Edgar Hayes, called.

"Terrific piece today," he said. "Keep up the good work."

Wait. I have one more screwdriver story. I was in spring training with the Tigers and my wife, back home, was sick for a week with the flu. I'd call and she could barely speak into the phone.

She would say, "Everything is fine. Don't worry about me."

I could hear a banging in the background—bang, bang, bang. A neighbor told me later it was my oldest son, who had been sent to his room for some reason or another, and now he was hammering on the door with his baseball bat.

I called on a Friday night and my wife sounded well. Almost a miracle recovery. She was upbeat and laughing and I could hear no banging in the background.

I felt so exhilarated I went to the press room and had three Michelobs. Hi, Tom.

We went out with manager Bob Scheffing. It was myself, Scheffing and Doug Mintline of the *Flint Journal.* Scheffing had been into the sauce himself and on the way over to a rib joint, he ran over the grass median on the highway, with the car flying into the air. Who cared? Nothing could harm us on this night.

I started in on the screwdrivers when we got there. One. Two. Three. Each with less orange juice and more vodka. I don't remember eating or going home.

The next morning I woke up and could not stand the smell. When I opened my eyes, I could not stand the sight. I had thrown up in every part of the room—including the bed.

We were to play an exhibition game in Orlando but my stomach was on fire. I called the room maid and offered her $50 if she would clean the room. She seemed very excited at making so much money. I left, feeling very sick but very lucky.

That was 1962, and it was the last time I had a drink.

Finally, there is John Gugger, present columnist at *The Toledo Blade*. He is as good a friend as I have in the business. The only thing I don't like about John is that he outwrites me. He certainly takes far more care in writing his column than I do. When we stay together, I can be done in 20 minutes. John polishes his pieces again and again. John Gugger is in his 50s and has as good a mind as any writer in the business today. (You owe me breakfast, lunch and dinner, John).

One problem with air travel is that you can't get close to the players. You may sit right across the aisle from them but they are usually caught up into reading, playing cards, working on private business, eating or sleeping. It is not easy to interrupt them.

Which brings us to the matter of talking off the record.

Most people in sports think if they talk off the record, they can tell you things but you can't use them. What good does that do? Your hands are tied. If you use it, you break a trust. If you don't use it, somebody else might find out about it and you are beaten on a story.

When someone wants to talk off the record, I tell them what off the record means to me: I'll listen to what they say but I won't quote them. And I won't use their comments unless I can get them confirmed by another reliable source. Surprisingly, nobody has ever objected to this method of operation.

And then we have Sparky Anderson. He'll talk morning, noon and night, always in a helpful and colorful manner. All you'd have to do is ask him something. He disliked the radio guys who held microphones in front of his face and never asked a question. He would push their microphones away and say, "If you don't have anything to ask, you're not going to feed off these other guys."

Anderson would talk about anything. Like how he spent each day as a manager.

He had an exact routine.

He'd get up by nine in the morning and eat breakfast in the coffee shop, usually waffles. He must have eaten waffles six out of seven days. He'd take a walk with Ernie Harwell, then back to his room for some phone calls, and back to bed for a nap. Turn off the phone, turn off the lights, sleep for a couple of hours. Out to the ball park by one o'clock in the afternoon and talk to the guards, the janitors, any workers who might be around at that hour. Anderson had time for them all.

After the games, he'd sit in bed and make out his lineup for the next day. But he had to have the TV on.

"I can't think unless the TV is on," he'd say.

Sparky liked to sit around the hotel pools, especially on off days. I asked him if he'd rate the swimming pools in the majors:

1. San Diego: "The best pool and the best scenery and I don't mean the mountains."
2. Houston: "A great place to sweat. Bring a pail of ice water because it will melt in 10 minutes and you can start drinking the water."
3. St. Louis: "Excellent. They sell hot dogs at pool side."
4. Pittsburgh: "Outstanding. The pool is on the roof of the hotel, 26 floors up, and you can catch the rays before they get down to the poor people below."
5. Kansas City: "Very restful, but you don't dare go to sleep because you might start snoring, and if you start snoring, your mouth opens and the players will start dingle-dangling things in your mouth."
6. Philadelphia: "A superb setting. They've got three pop machines at poolside and one of them sells Mr. Pibb. The record is three Mr. Pibbs in one day."

I asked him, how about the water? He said, "I never go near the water."

Sparky was probably the most popular manager in baseball. When he came to town, you always got a story from him. He was very polite, very accommodating, and always had something to say, whether or not you understood him.

I kept track of my favorite comments:

"I think firemen and what they do for a living, they're the real heroes in this world. We get paid outstanding money in baseball and people ask for our autographs, but who are we kidding? We're not the heroes. When you go to banquets and see mothers and fathers out there with the kids, they're the heroes because they care so much about their children."

"Whenever I eat right after a game, it's because I'm angry. I know if I don't do something, I can say some nasty things—so I eat to keep my mouth full."

"The biggest mistake people make is when they bad-mouth people after they're fired. Once you bad-mouth people, you can't bring it back."

"I hear guys complaining about where they sit on airplanes. I don't get it. Will they get there faster if they sit in a different seat?"

"To me, there is nothing wrong with having a good debate with an umpire as long as you don't curse him. If you start cursing the man, you should be gone."

"The only thing a manager can do once the game starts is to make moves with his pitchers, and you're going to be good at that only if you have good pitchers."

"I can understand people who boo us. You take a man who goes to the ball park—that's no different than paying for a show. You expect to get entertainment, and he's upset if he doesn't get it. I don't blame him."

"Some of the new ball parks are like plastic. They're beautiful, but you're not in contact with the fans. If I see a friend, I have to jump up to shake hands with him."

"I don't mind fans yelling at us, as long as they don't shoot bullets. Bullets are serious."

"I like to paint. Life should be like painting. If you see something you don't like, you paint right over it and it looks wonderful."

"The reason I keep my head down after changing pitchers is because the guy who is screaming at me might be my neighbor, and I don't want to know it."

Anderson was in demand wherever he went—summer, winter, autumn and spring. I asked him how he was able to handle the pressures of publicity on the road.

This time, he gave me this:

1.   Order room service whenever possible. Don't eat in any of the public dining rooms in the hotel.
2.   Don't answer the phone. Live by the message light on your phone. Call down for the messages and don't answer any of them unless they seem urgent.
3.   Don't lounge around in the lobby. Stay in your room as much as possible. Watch TV, play cards, nap, study algebra.
4.   Don't be rude to people, but keep walking if they besiege you for autographs.
5.   Don't miss the team bus.

And, finally, I asked him for the most memorable questions put to him:

1. "Did you have white hair at birth?"
2. "Do you plan to pose for Penthouse?"
3. "Who is going to win the Stanley Cup?"
4. "Would you buy a used car from yourself?"
5. "Did you ever hit one over the Berlin Wall?"
6. "Do you believe in belly buttons?"
7. "Are you voting for Reagan or Gromyko?"
8. "What is your favorite color?"
9. "Are you allergic to ivy?"
10. "Do you fill your pipe with Early American Rosin Bag?"

You would never know these things unless you traveled around with a ball club. I guess it was all worthwhile.

Except that near-miss in Minneapolis.

Chapter 6:
Joe D. and Darling Denny

My biggest scoop? Easy. It was the trade of managers, Jimmy Dykes for Joe Gordon, in 1960. I had the story, cold.

It was August and the Tigers were struggling. They were to finish in sixth place. We were in New York and you could feel a change of managers was imminent. It was just something in the air.

The Tigers were playing a twi-night doubleheader with the Yankees. I kept snooping around before the games, during the games and between the games. My office was expecting a strong story from me. I wasn't sure what was going on. I had no real information, so I decided to take my best guess: Dykes out and third base coach Billy Hitchcock in as interim manager.

Bad guess, Joe.

This is what I wrote—and this is what I went to bed with. I'd done my best, which wasn't quite good enough.

The phone in my hotel room rang at about 2 a.m. It was Mo Siegel, the veteran writer, calling from Washington.

"I've got one for you," he said.

I was still trying to wake up.

He said, "How about a trade of managers—Dykes for Gordon?"

I was awake that quick. "What? Say that again."

"Your team is going to trade Jimmie Dykes for Joe Gordon. The two teams are going to announce it at 10 o'clock this morning."

It sounded implausible. Nobody traded managers. Ever.

"I got it from Nate Dolan of the Indians," Siegel said. Dolan was one of the chief executives of the Indians and Mo said he was out drinking with him.

"It's true—go with it," said Siegel. "It's all yours."

I quickly called my office. I was with *The Detroit Times*, which was an afternoon paper, and our copy deadline was not until six o'clock in the morning. I told them what I had and went right to work on the story.

I wrote everything I could think of and knew it would make good reading—not because of my writing but because the story was so compelling. I could not wait until the 10 o'clock press conference.

I'd been having trouble with the front office over some of the things I'd written. I was like most young writers in those days—trying to draw attention to myself. I wrote some good stuff because I worked hard but sometimes I went a little too far and tried to be sensational.

Doc Fenkell, the club's publicity director, called the press conference in his room and the three writers traveling with the team—Sam Greene of *The News*, Hal Middlesworth of *The Free Press* and myself—showed up.

Fenkell leered at me as he held the publicity release in his hands.

"You're going to be surprised by this one," he said.

I had written my story on a typewriter and had a carbon copy in my jacket. I pulled it out and handed it to Doc. "You mean this one?" I said, trying not to leer.

He looked at it. The lead simply said, "Jimmy Dykes for Joe Gordon."

Poor Doc. He turned ashen. This was to be a special moment for him, a victory over the irritating guy from *The Times,* and now I had destroyed it all. I don't recall what he said but I do remember that puzzled look on his face.

I felt good, and bad. Good that I'd had the story, bad that I'd beaten Sam Greene so bad. He was my afternoon paper rival. More than that, he was my mentor, my idol—one of the finest men I have ever known. Sam was in his 60s and was a gentleman, a man of great dignity. He taught me how to behave on the baseball beat. He did it by example. If we got to the Kenmore Hotel in Boston, the manager would make a big fuss over our manager, saying how good it was to see him again. They had cookies and apples waiting for the players. Sam was always off to the side, talking to the bellhops or the elevator operators or the porters and the maids. He always took off his hat when he spoke to them—a true Southern gentleman.

Now, I had embarrassed him. Sam went to the phone, right there in Doc's room, and dictated a few paragraphs. I imagined how that would look compared to my eight-column headline on page one.

When I got back to the room, I called my office. Ed Hayes, the boss, answered the phone.

"Well, what do you think?" I asked.

"About what?" he said.

"My story...the trade of managers."

"We don't have a story about any trade of managers. Just your piece on Billy Hitchcock becoming the interim manager."

Talk about trying to handle a difficult moment.

The desk did not believe my story. Nobody traded managers. They put it on the spike and went with Hitchcock.

My greatest scoop. Down the drain.

For years, I thanked Mo Siegel for helping me. I never told him that my paper didn't run the story. Mo is gone—a good friend—so I guess it's OK to talk about it.

How about getting beaten by your own story? It happened when I was with The AP in Detroit. I was covering a Michigan-Missouri football game in the 1950s when Ron Kramer had a great day for the Michigan team. Don Faurot, the longtime and respected coach of the Missouri team, told me Kramer was the best tight end he had ever seen. I had an exclusive story since nobody else was around to hear his words.

When I sent my story in from Ann Arbor, my office in Detroit put it at the bottom of the pile of copy that was being sent to the outstate papers—the ones I was writing for that day. This was OK because the stories of the games had to go ahead of any side stories, such as mine.

We were located in the *Free Press* building and the copy boy from the *Free Press* came into our office and picked up our carbon copies of what we were sending on the state wire. The *Free Press* sports department saw my story about Kramer, took my byline off it (this was allowed), and ran it eight columns wide at the top of an inside sports page.

The *Free Press* papers started rolling off the presses at about 6:30 and The UPI, my rival which was situated across the street, got a copy at about 7 o'clock. They saw the Kramer story, figuring it was a *Free Press* piece, and quickly rewrote it and put it on their state wire.

Mine still hadn't moved on our wire.

The next day—a Sunday—the UPI beat us 9-0 in the outstate papers on the Kramer story. It was nobody's fault, just a quirk of our business.

A lot of crazy stuff happened at *The Detroit Times*. That's because we were always looking for stories. Every day of his life, Ed Hayes would come into the office and say, "You know what would make a good story...?"

Ed wasn't a very good writer but he was an excellent reporter. He had contacts everywhere.

The Yankees came to town and Mickey Mantle drove one out of the ball park. This was 1956—the first time it had happened since Ted Williams did it in 1939 (not at the 1941 All-Star game, as many believed. That one hit the third deck. He put one all the way out in a regular game in 1939. Now, two balls had sailed into Trumbull Ave.).

Mantle's shot took one bounce off the roof, near the light tower in right center, and disappeared from sight. It was a very big story in our town.

I got an idea. The next day we asked Al Kaline if he would go into his fielder's pose and stand along the third base line, in front of the Detroit dugout. Our photographer got into the dugout and shot up at Kaline. Then he took a picture of the rightfield roof.

We went back to the office and brought both pictures to our artist and asked him if he could reduce Kaline in size and place him in front of the roof in his fielding position. He said it would be no problem—give him a couple of hours and he'd have it for the next day's paper.

We would call it, "The Mantle Shift."

And there it was, as large as life, anchored on the upper lefthand part of the sports page—Al Kaline standing on the edge of the rightfield roof in Briggs Stadium, ready for anything Mantle might hit his way that night.

John McHale, Sr., was running the Tigers and when he saw the picture, he got right on the phone and called John Manning, editor of *The Detroit Times*. Manning was a warm and wonderful man and an outstanding newspaperman. McHale was screaming at him: "How dare you take our best player and put him on the edge of the roof!"

Mr. Manning was baffled. He hadn't seen the paper yet and did not know what McHale was talking about. He said he would look into it.

Manning called Hayes to his office. Edgar brought the sports section with him.

Manning murmured something like, "Do you think this was a very wise thing to do...Mr. McHale is quite upset and I'm not sure if I can blame him."

Edgar started laughing. "It's all a joke—a gag," he said. Edgar explained what we had done. Now, Mr. Manning was smiling. He liked a little spice in his newspaper.

He called McHale back and told him what had happened. McHale listened, then said, "OK...but don't ever take any of my players up there again."

The Tigers were looking for a manager after the trade of managers. Joe Gordon took one look at the pitiful players on the Tigers and quit at the end of the season. In fact, he closed the door to his downtown apartment after the final game and wouldn't open it for anyone.

Ed Hayes said one day: "I've got the new manager. It's going to be Bill Rigney. The deal is all set. I got it from Kenyon Brown." Brown was one of the 11 owners of the Tigers.

I wondered how Edgar got all this wonderful stuff. I didn't have a clue who the next manager was going to be.

He said, "You write it."

Me? It was his story, not mine.

But if Edgar had the dope, I guess I could do the rest.

I had nothing to go on but his word, so I went ahead and hired Rigney for two years. I paid him $30,000 a year. I never thought to call him on the phone. After all, Edgar was never wrong.

I still have a copy of that paper hanging in my den: "Rigney Named Tiger Manager." The date was October 27, 1960. The Tigers hired Bob Scheffing and a short while later, our paper went out of business. I could not get mad at Edgar. He was always trying to find stories and this time he missed.

The Yankees came to town another time. They were an explosive team. The best in baseball. I thought it would make a good layout if we got a picture of every Yankee who crossed the plate that night and run these pictures across the top of the sports section.

They scored 16 runs but I never told our photographer what I had in mind. I kicked myself as each run scored. The next day, I told Edgar of my goof, how I'd really blown a good layout.

"Do it tonight," he said.

"Come on, Edgar. They got 16 runs last night. It's not going to happen again."

He said, "Tell our photographer. I like the idea."

That night the Yankees scored 17 runs and the paper looked terrific the next day.

On my first trip north with the Tigers, we were winding up a weekend series in Houston and were to take the train on Sunday night to New Orleans. I was determined not to act like a rookie. I would watch what everyone else did and I would do the same. If they sent out their laundry, I'd send out my laundry. If they took cabs to the ball park instead of the team bus, I would take a cab.

We were to leave at about nine o'clock at night. That gave me time after the game to go back to my hotel room and write my story. I did a piece on how well Harvey Kuenn had hit that spring. They did not give us any statistics in those days, so I went back through my scorebook and wrote down all of his hits and all of his at bats. I thought it made a pretty good piece.

But now I had to get to the train station. I didn't want to be late. I put the story into my jacket pocket and got there with about a half hour to spare. I talked to the guys on the platform and felt pretty good about myself.

The next morning, in New Orleans, I was having breakfast at a hotel with Hal Middlesworth of *The Free Press* when I could hear a page in the lobby: "Joe Falls! Paging Joe Falls!"

I could feel a chill go through my body. I knew exactly what it was; it was my office calling. I opened my suit jacket and there it was, my story from the night before. I'd forgotten to bring it to Western Union so they could send it to Detroit.

I went to the phone and said, softly: "Hello. This is Joe. Who am I talking to?"

"It's Edgar. Are you all right?"

"I'm fine but..."

"Are you really OK?"

"I'm sorry, Edgar. I just forgot to file the story."

"That's OK," he said. "I just wanted to see if you were all right."

From that day on, this man could have had anything he wanted from me. We remained friends through all the years after our paper went out of business and I cannot tell you how many times I called on him when I was in a jam.

I've probably written more baseball than any other sport. That's because the seasons are so long and the Tigers have had some pretty good teams over the years.

But I like the game everywhere.

One day I thought Willie Mays' career was coming to an end and I had never written about him—never spoken to him. I could not let that happen. I flew to Cincinnati just to see him. He was a tough interview, so everyone said, and it was with some trepidation when I called his room at the hotel and asked if I could come up to see him.

I told him why I was there—that I'd made the trip just to see him—and he must have liked the idea.

He said, "Come ahead."

He gave me two hours of his time and I got a neat story.

Time passed. I took my young son to Cooperstown to see the Hall of Fame. I thought he would enjoy it. A mistake. He was only 12 years old and these were not his heroes, they were mine. He knew nothing about them. So as I rummaged around the place for two days, my son went fishing. He got a tree branch and found some string and a safety pin and made himself a fishing pole. He caught 78 fish one day, 72 the next. He threw them all back.

On the final day, I made him come into the Hall of Fame building with me. If nothing else, I wanted him to see Jackie Robinson's locker. They had a special display for him, his Brooklyn uniform with the blood-red No. 42 on the front, in a locker from Ebbets Field.

When I took him up to the exhibit, I whispered, "Do you know who that is?"

My son said, "Doesn't he play for the Baltimore Orioles?"

"No, that's Frank Robinson. This is Jackie Robinson. He played for the Brooklyn Dodgers."

My son shrugged.

I leaned in closer and said, "He was the first black player in baseball."

Again, no reaction.

I leaned in even closer. "You know, there was a time when they didn't allow black players in baseball."

My son spun around and looked at me. He said, "That's dumb. They're the best players."

I had my story for that day.

We went on to New York for an oldtimer's game in Shea Stadium. I've always had a rule as a writer—I never brought my kids into the dressing rooms, dugouts, anywhere they shouldn't be. Some guys do it; I didn't. If they wanted to hang out on their own and get autographs, fine. But they were not getting any special privileges just because dad was a sports writer.

When we got to Shea Stadium, I told my son to wait for me in a hallway outside the dressing room while I went inside to see the players. As I walking around the dressing room, Joe DiMaggio came up to me and said, "May I shake your hand?"

I looked around. Was he talking to me?

"I'd like to shake your hand," he repeated.

I stuck out my hand and he shook it warmly. "I just want to thank you for all the nice things you've written about me in my career."

I had written many things about this man, much of it in *The Sporting News,* but I never thought about him reading it. I was thrilled.

Just then, I looked around the room and who should be sitting in front of one of the lockers but my son, Mike.

"What are you doing here? How'd you get in here?"

Before he could answer, Mays walked up. He said, "He's my guest. I brought him in."

More confusion in my mind.

"I saw him out there in the hallway and asked his name," said Mays. "When he told me he was Joe Falls' son, I knew I couldn't leave him out there. I told him of the time his father flew all the way from Detroit to Cincinnati just to see me. That was a special day for him and I thought I would make this a special day for him."

Talk about going two-for-two...

When DiMaggio turned 70, I thought I would call him up and do a story. It seemed like the proper thing to do. I had read when his birthday was going to be and I got his number from a friend in Philadelphia, Ed Libatore, an old scout. He knew me from *The Sporting News,* so he gave me DiMaggio's number in San Francisco.

I called and he was very pleased. We chatted for about a half hour. As we were saying goodbye, he said, "You're the only one to call me today."

That made me feel bad. Joe D., 70, and nobody called. I did not mention this in my story but it troubled me for a long time.

The next spring, I went over to Winter Haven, training camp of the Boston Red Sox, for my annual visit with Ted Williams. These were some of the best days of my life. I could not believe a kid off the streets of New York, who always watched from a distance, never troubling the players for autographs, could sit and talk baseball with one of the greatest hitters of all time.

Williams took me to dinner one night, and it was memorable. We went to a Chinese restaurant and he wouldn't even let me look at the menu. He ordered for both us—stuff I'd never heard of—and it was marvelous.

When we were done, he got up and said: "I'm a chocoholic. Did you know that I'm one of the great chocoholics in this country?"

He drove to Howard Johnson's and ordered two specials—brownies and chocolate ice cream, covered with chocolate sauce. I only mention this because I was never more honored in my life.

I told him of my call to DiMaggio, how he gave me a half hour of his time, and how much that meant to me. These two were great competitors for years—the Yankee Clipper with that 56-game hitting streak and The Kid with that .406 batting average, both in 1941. They were men of great pride—men who always tried to outdo the other, but in a quiet way.

"Yep," I told Williams, "a whole half hour."

We talked of many things and when I was leaving, walking across one of the minor league fields, Williams yelled after me: "Hey, Bush!"

I turned around.

He pointed at me and said, "You be sure to call me on my 70th birthday. I'll give you an hour."

I was a baseball writer for 10 years—five at *The Detroit Times* and five at *The Free Press.* In this time, I became an official scorer and felt it was a badge of honor. They paid us $50 a game but I didn't do it for that reason. I did it because this is how I thought you became a well-rounded baseball writer.

I would never do it again—not for $5,000 a game. It is too much battling with the players. No one ever says you did a good job of scoring, but make one mistake or even a questionable call—and whammo! You are into it with them after the games. Instead of working on your story, you are arguing with them.

Baseball should not allow writers to be official scorers. They should hire other people, maybe retired umpires, but that would mean they'd have to pay them some decent money, and for all the dough the game brings in, the owners have never felt this was an important consideration.

Anyway, I got into the Hall of Fame through my official scoring.

This was in 1962. The Tigers and Yankees were playing a Sunday game in Detroit. It started at 1:30 p.m. and ended at 8:30 p.m. It was the longest game in the history of baseball.

They went 22 innings that day—June 24. The Yankees finally won 9-7 on a two-run homer by Jack Reed (his only homer in the majors) but not before the 35,638 fans consumed 32,000 hot dogs, 41,000 bottles of beer and 34,500 bottles of pop.

They played so long that the Michigan labor laws made them shut down the concession stands at 8:15 because women were not permitted to work more than 10 hours on a Sunday.

Matt Dennis, a sports writer for the *Windsor Star,* got up from his seat in the press box in the 18th inning and announced, "I've got to leave, my visa just expired."

Barney Lorrey, a taxi driver, pulled up at the stadium at 4:30 and waited for a fare. He got one four hours later.

The old record was five hours and 19 minutes, so they shattered that mark by one hour and 41 minutes. As the game ended, the clock in centerfield read 8:29. I did not want a time of six hours and 59 minutes. I wanted the magic figure of seven hours. So I paused for a moment before picking up the microphone in the press box. I cleared my throat a few times and when I thought enough time had passed, I announced: "Time of game, seven hours."

Everybody cheered.

In later years, Jerry Greene, one of my colleagues at *The News,* said I had cheated an entire minute. Good old Jerry. He could find fault anywhere. He was never an official scorer.

One day, I was scoring a game in Detroit and Jerry was sitting next to me. Rocky Colavito, my arch enemy, hit an easy fly to right. Sam Bowens, the Baltimore rightfielder, butchered the play. He ran under the ball and it fell behind him.

"That's got to be an error," said Jerry.

I picked up the mike and said, "E-9."

You can imagine how it went in the dressing room after the game. Colavito came after me. Nobody had touched the ball, so how could it be an error? He was furious. He also didn't know the rule book.

I was in manager Charlie Dressen's office when he tore into the room, picked me up out of my chair and held me against the wall by my throat. That was bad enough but my feet weren't touching the ground.

Dressen, a small man, pulled Colavito off me. He said, "Hey, you can't kill the guy."

Oh, no? You should have seen the look on The Rock's face.

In any case, the Hall of Fame called the next day about the seven-hour game. They wanted my box score, my story and my picture for a special display. The next spring, Kenny Smith, a former New York baseball writer who worked for the Hall of Fame, came to the Tigers' camp and wanted my voice describing what happened on that wild day. They wanted to add it to their exhibit.

Kenny figured my place was fixed forever in the lore and legend of the game. I tended to agree. I said to everyone who would listen (or even if they wouldn't listen), "Who is the only active baseball writer in the Hall of Fame."

I never let up.

Not until two seasons later, on May 31, 1964, when the New York Mets and San Francisco Giants played a 23-inning game at Shea Stadium that lasted seven hours and 23 minutes and the curators of Cooperstown took down:

My box score...

My story...

My picture...

My voice...

And put them all into a small box and stored them in the basement.

I had more adventures as an official scorer. Bud Daly was pitching for the Kansas City A's and early in the game there was a close play at first base. The shortstop had juggled the ball for a moment and the runner was called safe. I ruled it a base hit on the belief the play was too hard to handle.

That was the only hit going into the ninth inning and Daly kept glaring up at the press box. I knew I had to talk to him after the game —rip me if he wanted—because it was the only fair way to do it. I did not look forward to that prospect, however.

Daly got the first out in the ninth and there it was again: an awful scowl up into the press box.

I said to myself: "Come on, somebody get a hit. Please. Just one teeny-weeny single."

And, lo, my prayers were answered.

The next two batters got clean hits and I was off the hook. I did not go down to see Mr. Daly, but I have not forgotten that expression on his face.

Another time Bob Bruce was pitching for the Tigers. The batter swung at a pitch far out of the strike zone and struck out. The ball got past the catcher and the batter reached first.

I called it a wild pitch, meaning Bruce, not the catcher, was responsible for the runner, who eventually came around to score. It put one more earned run on his record.

Ring. Ring.

It was Bruce calling the press box. At first, I couldn't understand him. He was yelling too loud. When he calmed down a bit, he wanted to know how-in-hell-could-I-call-a-wild-pitch-when-the-batter-swung-at-the-ball-and-missed?

I told him it didn't matter if the batter swung or not; the ball was still away outside and it was a wild pitch. I don't remember his reaction but he was a good guy and never mentioned it again and we got along fine.

Rich Shook, formerly of the UPI, called one against Tony Phillips of the Tigers and Phillips stopped in back of the plate and glared up Richie. He was trying to show him up. Fine. No law against that.

Later, in the dressing room, Phillips called Richie all kinds of names, none of them flattering, and I wrote a piece saying that Phillips was out of line with this kind of behavior. Nobody had ever spoken to Phillips that way and he had no right to speak to anyone else in such a manner.

That made Phillips even madder.

He cornered me in the dugout the next day and went at me for a long time. I listened, then went back at him. I could see we were not going to resolve our differences, and what made it especially hard on me is that Richie wasn't upset by what Phillips had said. I was left out on a limb, but kept hanging on.

Finally, Phillips and I started taking about other things, baseball in general, and we both seemed glad to get off the subject of Richie's call. The conversation went on for another 30 minutes and we shook hands at the end of it. Since that moment, my esteem for this man has gone away up. He had his say but was not willing to make a federal case of it. I wish more players could be as sensible. We are not perfect but neither are they.

My pet peeve is that too many players think they should get the calls at home because the other teams get them in their own ball parks. Sad to say, there are too many hometown scorers who do this. They don't want to face the wrath of these players. If I was scoring again, I'd call them as I saw them and wear heavy armor to the ball park.

One more thing: this business of saying the first hit has to be a good hit if a pitcher is working on a no-hitter is nonsense. A hit is a hit and an error is an error. The biggest problem I found is that some plays are 50-50. They could go either way. Those are the toughies. My toughest call was a ball hit at the third baseman's feet where the ball bounces into the air. It happens so quickly that it's hard to tell whether he should have had it or not. That, and low passed balls. How can you tell where the ball is if you are so far from the play?

Again, not for $5,000 a game. (Maybe $10,000).

Now to Rocky Colavito . . .

No player ever disliked me more than this man. He had been a big hero in Cleveland--almost a God to the fans. Don't Knock The Rock. They simply loved this man and worshipped at his altar. He was tall, dark and handsome and could hit home runs. So, he struck out and couldn't run so well, so what? He smiled and signed autographs for everyone. And that smile...he was everybody's favorite.

I was sitting in the press box in Lakeland on the final day of the 1960 spring training season when Rick Ferrell walked in during the ninth inning. He was the general manager of the Tigers and looked as if he had seen a ghost.

He leaned over and, in a very shaky voice, said, "We've traded Harvey Kuenn for Rocky Colavito."

Poor Rick. He could barely get the words out.

I spun around in my seat and looked at the clock. It was after four. I had only a couple of hours to write the story, and I knew the impact it would create.

The batting champion for the home run champion. It doesn't get much bigger. Kuenn had batted .353 and Colavito had hit 42 home runs the previous year.

I worked until midnight on the story but the real fun didn't start until the next day. As it happened, the Tigers were opening in Cleveland and the two players would face each other in the first game of the season.

The trade had been made by Bill Dewitt, boss of the Tigers, and Frank (Trader) Lane of the Indians. Both men were somewhat egotistical. When we got to Cleveland, Lane was popping off all over the place about how he had put one over the Tigers.

There was a tremendous outcry from the fans—how could Lane do such a thing? This was The Rock. Our Rock. How dare he send him away? Lane said, "What's the big deal—I traded a hamburger for a steak."

That did it. All the phones lit up in the Cleveland front office, as well as at radio and TV stations. This was intolerable. This was anarchy. This was war.

The fans started turning out early for the game. Some came with ropes to lynch Lane. The early arrivals filled up the rightfield seats. That's where The Rock would be playing. They wanted to be as close to him as possible, a teary farewell to a great man.

I never felt more electricity in a ball park than that day in Cleveland. I thought the fans might set the stadium on fire.

The game went 15 innings, into the darkness, before Al Kaline shot a single into center to win it for the Tigers. Poor Rocky. He struck out four times, popped up and hit into a double play. He was 0-6.

By the time it ended, it was pretty cold and most of the fans had gone home, leaving the rightfield sector looking like a garbage dump. The signs were shattered, ripped into pieces and flying around the field. The banners were gone. Hardly anyone was left. Casey, Mighty Casey, had struck out.

When the Tigers got back to Detroit, Colavito hit a three-run homer into the upper deck in left-center on opening day and everyone went crazy. But nothing could wipe away that frustrating moment in Cleveland. While Colavito was a good player for the Tigers, he was never idolized in Detroit the way he was in Cleveland.

I didn't help matters by poking fun at him. I did not realize he was so sensitive, so I wrote things like, "The Tigers have Colavito in left because he has the feet for it." I got that one from Larry Middlemas of *The Detroit News* but never told anyone.

The thing that infuriated The Rock more than anything is that I kept count of his RNBIs—Runs Not Batted In. He got a lot of RBIs but I also sensed he was leaving a lot of runners on base. So, whenever he stranded runners at second and third, I would add up the figures and put them in my story.

What finally set him off against me was what happened in spring training. Colavito was holding out. He reported to Lakeland but refused to sign his contract. He was offered something like $52,500 while Al Kaline was at $55,000. The Rock wanted more dough than Kaline but General Manager Jim Campbell wouldn't give it to him. Campbell held firm at $52,500. He felt the honor belonged to Kaline, who had been the star of the team for nearly 10 years.

Norm Cash was also holding out. He was living at the same motel as Colavito and they set up their own mini-camp, running and playing catch every day. When I heard of it, I took our photographer, Dick Tripp, and we went out there and hid in the bushes. Dick got some neat pictures of them throwing the ball back and forth and the story ran at the top of our sports page the next day.

Cash thought it was hilarious; Colavito wanted to kill me. Around and around it went for several years, me having my fun and The Rock having his fits.

I never allowed my kids around the ball club, but one day we went to St. Petersburg for an exhibition game with the Yankees. I got there early to talk to as many people as I could. My son sat in the stands by himself.

A little later when I looked into the Detroit dugout, guess who was sitting there—none other than Bobby Falls.

"What are you doing here?"

"I don't know," he said. "Mr. Blackburn (Wayne Blackburn, a Tiger scout) saw me sitting in the stands and asked if I wanted to be the bat boy."

Blackburn did not know Bobby was my son, so I had to let him stay on the bench. I told him, "OK, just do a good job."

Bobby did such a good job that they made him the bat boy for the rest of the spring. You can figure out who adopted him as if he was his own son. My good friend Rocco Dominico Colavito. If The Rock couldn't get to me, he would do it through my son. He treated him royally, showing Bobby what a great guy he was.

Bobby would tell me: "Boy, that Mr. Colavito is a nice man. He gave me some ice cream today and some soda pop during the game."

They had a father-and-son game that summer and the only way I could get back at Colavito was to put a press card in my son's hat and send him into the dugout to interview Rocky, Jr.

The Rock finished his career in Detroit and we still didn't talk.

As the years passed, he retired from the game and became a coach with the Indians. They were in town to play the Tigers and I figured, "Why not?" I called him at his hotel in downtown Detroit.

When he answered the phone, I said, "Colavito. This is Falls. I'm coming over and cleaning your clock."

He said, "You come right ahead, Mr. Falls. I'll be waiting for you."

I went over to the Sheraton Hotel and knocked on his door. He opened it and we looked at each other and smiled. He said, "Weren't we assholes—a couple of juveniles?"

We hugged and spent the rest of the afternoon laughing over our childish ways. This is a good man and I often think of him, hoping his life as a mushroom farmer in Pennsylvania is a happy one.

The Tigers had a first baseman named Bob Farley. He wasn't very good, and I said so in my column. He got so upset he called my home and said I not only was ruining his life but the lives of his wife and children. I thought he was overdoing it but it was unsettling to hear such comments. I did not feel proud of myself.

The worst, though, was a player who I will not name because we are friends and I don't want to damage our friendship. But he truly scared me one day after I'd written a critical piece about him. He said, "I'm not going to do anything to you but I can't speak about my brothers. And you know how they are."

That was a real chiller. Nothing ever happened. What was so strange is that this player was one of the sweetest guys ever to play for the Tigers. It told me that words can be hurtful, so be careful how you use them.

I was 19 and living in New York when Jackie Robinson was brought up by the Brooklyn Dodgers in 1947, the first black player in the majors. My buddies and I were big baseball fans, our loyalties divided among the Yankees, Giants and Dodgers. We didn't think much of Robinson's appearance. I lived in an all-white neighbor-hood and went to an all-white high school, so I wasn't involved with black people. My father used to take me to Yankee Stadium all the time. He was a New York City policeman and got in free. He even rode the subways free. All he had to pay for was my ticket and a nickel each way on the train. We'd always go to the doubleheaders on Sunday—first the Yankees, then the Black Yankees. I never thought much of that, either. It was just what we did. I saw all the black teams play and enjoyed the games. The only difference was I was never sure who was playing for the Black Yankees because the news-papers never wrote about these games. They seemed to play as good as the White Yankees.

So when Robinson came along, it was nothing special to us. I wasn't mature enough to understand all the social ramifications. All we knew was that Robinson was a terrific player. We'd never seen one like him. He was quick, he was fast, he was daring. He'd drive the other teams nuts by the way he ran the bases. We were taken by him not because of his color but because of his ability. We'd never seen a player quite like him. The two best clutch hitters I ever saw in my life were Jackie Robinson and Yogi Berra.

I went through all the black players in Detroit. The first was Ozzie Virgil, and some didn't accept him as the real thing because he came from the Dominican Republic. This was in 1958. That was 11 years after Robinson had broken the color line and some people in Detroit maintained the Tigers drew a color line over the years. That may have been true but I never felt it. I certainly never heard anything like it around the ball park. I never heard one disparaging comment against black players. I assumed they just weren't good enough. I was new to my job and may have missed a lot of things.

If you would ask me today if the club was racially prejudiced, I would say no. Dumb, maybe. But not racist.

The Tigers were the 15th of 16 teams to sign a black player, the Boston Red Sox being last. In retrospect, that makes the Tigers look bad. They brought up Virgil when we were ending a road trip in Washington. He played third base and didn't do much. The story didn't cause much of a stir in the papers, either. The big moment came when they returned to Briggs Stadium. A fairly good-sized crowd turned out and Virgil could not have been more impressive. He went 5-for-5.

It so happened I was into a squabble with Bill Norman, the manager. He was a minor leaguer who was in over his head as a major league manager. A nice man but miscast. He thought he would get even with me by closing his clubhouse after Virgil's first appearance in Detroit. While the reporters and photographers waited outside, Virgil slipped out the side door and went into the night without talking to anyone.

Ozzie was a good guy who didn't enjoy all the fuss. He had a terrific sense of humor and we were always gagging around with each other. In fact, as the years passed, we would embrace whenever we met in our travels. He is one guy who has a genuine twinkle in his eye.

You have to be very careful what you write these days because the race issue has become so sensitive. I try not to think about it, but it is always in the corner of your mind. If somebody calls you a racist, what can you do about it? It may be wrong—unfair—but the brand is there, and somehow it stays.

I made up my mind I would treat everyone on their ability, sometimes on their decency. I would not let color into my thinking. But the problem was always there. I could say Steve Kemp, a white man, did not run out a grounder and it was okay. But if I said Lou Whitaker, a black man, did not run out a grounder, here would come the letters of protest.

In Lakeland, the New Florida Hotel, headquarters of the Tigers, would not accept black players, so General Manager Jim Campbell pulled his club out of there and set up at a nearby Holiday Inn. He thought that would solve the problem. Wrong.

While the black players stayed there, it was clear they were not comfortable. You could understand it. How could they overcome years of prejudice almost overnight? Impossible.

To make them feel welcome, Campbell had a special dining room set up for all the players. If the black players were uneasy in the main dining room, they now had their own place, with their own teammates, where they could enjoy their meals.

The white players didn't use the dining room, nor did the black players. The white players went to fancier places or ate in the homes they had rented. The black players went back to the neighborhoods where they had always been welcomed, eating and enjoying the company of their own people. Campbell tried but failed.

Jim used to get angry at any suggestion his team was racist in any way. The charge always came up because the Tigers did not have many black players. Campbell was not in charge when the Tigers did not sign blacks, and he resented any implication he was against any kind of minorities. I knew this man as well as I knew anyone in baseball and never felt he had a racist bone in his body.

Two of his favorite players were Willie Horton and Gates Brown, black men who came up the hard way—Horton from the streets of Detroit and Brown from a prison in Ohio. He treated them as if they were his sons and they looked to him as a father figure.

Gates would run short of dough in spring training and he'd go to Campbell for a "fast Jackson." That was a twenty dollar bill he would return as soon as he could. Sometimes, it would be a "slow Jackson." That took a little longer to pay back. When Campbell died in 1995, he left some money in his will so "Willie and Gates can have a party on me."

Among the first black players on the Tigers was outfielder Billy Bruton—I called him Billy B.—and second baseman Jake Wood. Bruton was special. He was such a quiet man, a gentleman, a man of rare intelligence. You could always go to him and get a meaningful comment. He was a skinny guy, a bag of bones, and the day he announced his retirement he filled the air with laughter. He was 36 at time.

"Thirty-six!" he howled. "I fooled you guys for years. I'm 39. I cheated three years on you and you didn't know it." Billy B.'s picture hangs in my den.

What made Wood special is he was my son's favorite player. Wood would strike-out all the time—141 times in his rookie year to set an American League record. It didn't matter. Bobby just loved the man—that laconic, laid-back man who had his own quite sense of humor.

My other son, Mike, 14 years younger than his older brother, also had a favorite player. He was Tony Taylor, another black who came over from the National League. Don't ask me why he liked Taylor, but he did, and I'd better not say anything wrong or write anything wrong about him.

Pitcher Earl Wilson was one of my favorites. He was a big guy who came to the Tigers from the Boston Red Sox. He was the first player to have an agent, which sort of stunned Jim Campbell, but Earl never made a big deal out of it. The agent was the late Bob Woolf of Boston. What I'll never forget is the day the team was leaving for St. Louis to start the 1968 World Series. Denny McLain called George Cantor, our baseball writer at *The Free Press*, a "bleeping Jewish bleeper" in a confrontation in the clubhouse. I went after Denny but before I could get to him, Wilson pulled me away. He said, "He's not worth it." Whenever we meet these days, I know what I am going to get from Earl Wilson—a big hug.

Dennis Dale McLain. Where do you begin with this man?

I was his Boswell, at least at the start. When the Tigers got him from the Chicago White Sox in 1963, he wasn't well known, except that Lou Boudreau, the old Cleveland shortstop and manager who was broadcasting for the Chicago Cubs, was his father-in-law. But I could spot a character when I saw one.

I noticed he was drinking Pepsi-Colas all day long. I asked about it and he said he was addicted, finishing off as many as 25 cans a day. That made a story. Then I found out about his organ playing ability and that made another off-beat piece. Finally, it was his flying. I wrote that, too, and now other people in the business started paying attention to this man. They liked characters, too.

When Denny started hitting it big on the field, he did not exactly turn away from me, but he didn't need me anymore—so I no longer had an in with him. This was OK with me because this is when he started getting into trouble—one bankruptcy, another bankruptcy, stiffing people all over the place, failing to pitch well at the end of the 1967 season when he hurt his foot and some felt the Mafia did it to him because he owed them money. I never knew what happened but it was clear that Denny was capable of a lot of things, some real, some imagined, all of interest to the public. He seemed to enjoy the attention, even when it wasn't favorable.

Denny was a great interview. If 10 guys went to his locker after a game, they'd come away with good stories—10 different stories. Denny would make them up as he went along and nobody seemed to care. It made great reading.

McLain had it all—fame, fortune, a fiery fast ball and 31 victories in 1968. He lost it all just two years later when he set the unbelievable record of being suspended three times in one season. No player in history ever squandered so much wealth and talent in a shorter time.

His woes began when *Sports Illustrated* printed in its February 23, 1970, issue the story of McLain's involvement in a Flint (Michigan) bookmaking operation in 1967. The title of the expose was "Baseball's Big Scandal—Denny McLain and the Mob." Denny was portrayed as being taken in—"poor, dumb Denny" the magazine called him—by the operators of the book, who billed him for the losses but somehow forgot to tell him of the winnings. To make matters worse, it was uncovered that McLain was making his own bets on basketball games and using the press room phone right in the Tiger clubhouse in Lakeland. He was indeed a brazen young man, placing his bets on one occasion in front of two newspapermen. One of these men was my good friend Doug Mintline of the *Flint Journal*. Doug knew this was big stuff but decided not to write it. He told manager Mayo Smith and Smith didn't do anything about it, either. Doug felt the way things were going with the Tigers—a championship season after the city had burned in the bloodiest, costliest riot in history during the 1967 season—it was not the time to bring up more trouble. Doug did not tell me this until years later. He always tried to rationalize his judgment. I didn't agree with him.

Four days before the *Sports Illustrated* expose hit the newsstands, McLain was summoned to Commissioner Bowie Kuhn's office in New York. Kuhn apparently got wind of what the magazine was about to reveal and wanted to get the facts himself. It was very much of a cloak-and-dagger operation. Jerry Green of *The Detroit News* was in New York and wandered into Kuhn's office and saw McLain. He said: "What are you doing here?" Jerry rode in a cab with McLain to the airport and wrote a compelling story for the next day's paper.

The magazine story and McLain's visit to the commissioner's office rocked the baseball world—a world that hadn't known a tinge of scandal for almost five decades. On February 19, Kuhn said he was indefinitely suspending McLain for his involvement in bookmaking.

Nobody knew how deeply Denny was in, not even the commissioner, and all sorts of speculation followed the suspension. McLain became the focal character on the nation's sports pages. Everyone wondered just what had he done—and what would baseball do to him. Kuhn launched a "full-scale investigation." McLain slipped back to his home in Lakeland and was told by his lawyers to say nothing to no one. But he talked to some media people because he simply couldn't shut up. Not his nature. This only added to the flames.

Eventually, McLain's tangled financial affairs became public. Though he had been earning $200,000 a year, his lawyers filed a bankruptcy petition in his behalf which listed a whopping debt of $446,069, of which $273,500 was the result of a variety of suits filed against him. Denny had his fingers in many pies.

McLain's "assets" were listed at $413, from which he was supposed to pay off 86 creditors. He was charging quite a few things, too, like diamond rings. Even the Tigers were burned by his free-spending ways. They were listed among his creditors to the sum of $39,386, which had been an advance on his 1970 salary.

This was a device Denny employed to borrow money, using his contract as collateral. The trouble was he borrowed more money than the contract was worth. On one occasion, he attempted to borrow $25,000 from a Detroit bank. The bank called the Tigers to see if his contract would cover the loan. The Tigers said no, but the bank put the loan through anyway. Denny McLain's name was very powerful in Detroit.

On March 19, a month after his suspension, the furniture in McLain's rented home in Detroit was seized by the Internal Revenue Service to satisfy a tax bill amounting to $9,460. The IRS sold the furnishings at auction, bringing in $5,852. Included in the items was a Hammond organ, which McLain later said did not belong to him but was loaned to him by the company.

On April 1, Kuhn announced that McLain was being suspended until July 1 for "his involvement in reported bookmaking activities in 1967 and his associations at the time." Kuhn said his investigation had shown that McLain had not tampered with any ball games.

Most of the media thought Kuhn was too lenient. Catcher Bill Freehan of the Tigers said, "Half a season? It's like saying he almost did something wrong." The Tigers had expected McLain to be banished for the season and were relieved at his sentence.

McLain remained in Lakeland and was told to "clam up." When he returned on July 1, he was scheduled to start against the Yankees and a crowd of 53,863—the largest in Detroit in 19 years—turned out for the event. One fan's reaction was typical of others: "I don't care about his suspension, the bankruptcy or any of those things. I'm only interested in seeing that high, hard one again."

Writers from all over the country converged on Detroit. The crowd gave McLain a rousing reception. He said, "I thought I was going to cry when I heard all those cheers."

I could not believe what was going on.

McLain pitched 5$^1/_3$ innings. He left with the Tigers losing 5-3. Detroit rallied to win in extra innings but that was only incidental. Denny was back and again the world would be right in Detroit. He tried four more times without winning, then won two in a row. But it was not until his 13th start that he could go all the way.

Then the clouds started to gather again.

On August 28, Denny doused two Detroit sports writers with buckets of water. What a dummy. I was his biggest critic and he didn't get me. He got Jim Hawkins of *The Free Press* and Watson Spoelstra of *The News*. What I held against Denny is that he stiffed people twice with his bankruptcy bit. I felt this could happen to anyone one time, but when he did it a second time, it was malicious because it was done by design.

McLain said he was merely being playful with his water trick, but General Manager Jim Campbell suspended him for "a period not to exceed 30 days." It would cost Denny $500 a day, which he could not afford.

As it turned out, the suspension was for only seven days. It was to end on September 5. But on September 4, Kuhn was back in the picture. He asked the Detroit officials to come to New York and bring McLain with them. Again, Denny was placed under suspension, this time for carrying a gun and violating his probation. McLain had toted the gun during a road trip August 6-19 and, on at least one occasion, had shown it to some teammates in a Chicago restaurant.

The final chapter of Denny's story was written on October 9, the eve of the World Series in Cincinnati. Kuhn called the media together and with Campbell standing at his side, he announced the Tigers had traded McLain to the Washington Senators. Now the World Series was upstaged. It was the first time a commissioner had ever announced a trade. But this was a special deal since McLain was still under suspension.

Kuhn said that McLain had undergone a psychiatric examination—and had passed—before the trade was made.

Later, McLain told reporters: "I've got a piece of paper saying I'm sane. How about you guys?"

On the way back to his hotel after the press conference, Campbell threw a small object into the street and muttered, "I won't be needing these anymore."

It was a package of Tums.

The Denny McLain I knew and the Denny McLain others knew were two different people. That's because I never did any business with him. He never hurt me. He was the ultimate imp.

Here's what I saw in his big season of 1968 when he went 31-6 and pitched the Tigers into the World Series:

April 11: It's the second day of the season and Mickey Lolich, the No. 2 pitcher, is away on National Guard duty following the assassination of Dr. Martin Luther King. McLain gets the call. He is not involved in the decision but shows up with something new: a mop of red hair.

April 21: McLain wins his first game in his third start.

May 1: McLain runs his record to 3-0 by beating Minnesota. He retires Tony Oliva four straight times. He says, "If I pitch that way all the time, I'm going in and asking for a million dollars next season."

Harmon Killebrew and Rich Reese hit home runs off him and McLain says, "As far as I'm concerned, they can take this ball park and throw it into the Atlantic ocean."

He denies he has dyed his hair.

May 5: Denny runs his record to 4-0 and sounds off about the Detroit fans. With the writers jammed around his locker, he says, "Detroit has the biggest front-running fans in the world. Norm Cash and I were going bad last season and they got on us real bad. How do they think a guy's wife feels when he goes zero for eight or zero for sixteen and the fans boo him while she's in the stands? If they think we're stupid for playing this game, how stupid are they for watching us?"

Tom Loomis of the *Toledo Blade* shows up a little later and McLain tells him, "What I mean is that only one percent of the fans are stupid."

It is a little late. The story goes into all the other papers.

June 13: McLain wins his 10th game and the blond-brown crop of hair is back.

June 20: Denny loses a no-hitter in the seventh inning against Boston when the ball grazes off the glove of shortstop Ray Oyler. What did Denny say? "I said 'fudge.'"

July 3: Denny wins his 15th, then pronounces, "I don't consider myself the best pitcher in the league, only on the nights when I go out to pitch."

July 7: Denny runs his record to 16-2 in the first game of a doubleheader. He climbs up to the third level and serenades the fans on the organ during the second game.

July 10: It's the All-Star break in Houston. Denny flies in from Las Vegas, pitches two scoreless innings, then flies right back.

July 27: Denny wins his 20th in the midst of a Detroit newspaper strike. He says, "The big thing is the writers aren't around to demoralize the players."

July 31: Denny makes it No. 21 and says of Tiger Stadium, "I hate this place, I hate this place, I hate this place." A new organ is delivered to his home in the afternoon.

August 14: Denny wins No. 24 and reveals *Time* and *Newsweek* are closing in him. He says Ed Sullivan and Joey Bishop also want him on their TV shows. And he has an organ recital in New York.

August 19: It's the "Today Show" in New York, followed by a recital at the Hampshire House, followed by a meeting with his agent, Frank Scott.

August 20: Before he leaves New York, Denny tells Milt Richman of the UPI he has been pitching with a torn shoulder muscle. When he returns to Detroit, a writer asks him about the torn muscle. Denny says, "It's only torn to the extent that it's strained."

September 1: Denny starts a triple play against the Orioles, grabbing Boog Powell's liner at belt buckle level. On the plane to the West Coast that night, he tells everyone how lucky he is: "That ball was headed straight for my head. Good thing I got my glove up there or I could have been blinded." The next day, the newspapers showed him catching the ball at belly-button level.

September 9: Denny spends his day conferring with the Smothers Brothers and their TV staff. He says, "Their pad costs $40,000. I want one just like it..

September 14: This is the day Denny wins his 30th. He beats the Oakland A's. Catcher Jim Pagliaroni of the A's walks around the park carrying a sign "Dobson Going For No. 10 Today." Dizzy Dean shows up. He was the last pitcher to win 30 games. Watson Spoelstra of *The Detroit News* throws him out of the press box.

December 1: Denny is appearing in Las Vegas. He tells the audience: "I wouldn't trade 10 Mickey Loliches for one Bob Gibson. He realizes his blunder and walks out on the stage the next night and says the same thing: "I wouldn't trade a dozen Mickey Loliches for one Bob Gibson." The third night he gets it straight: "I wouldn't trade a dozen Bob Gibsons for one Mickey Lolich." Too late. The story is out, and Denny looks bad once again.

McLain had a good-natured way about him. For all the trouble he gave Campbell, Campbell liked him. He liked to tell the story about the day he was chewing Denny out in his office.

"I was giving it to him, big time," Campbell said. "I threatened him with everything I could think of. Denny never said a word. When he got up to leave, he stopped at the door and said, 'You know, I like your style. I might have a job for you in my paint company.'"

McLain kept messing around after he retired from the game and was sentenced to 23 years in prison for racketeering, money laundering and who knows what else. He had not learned a thing. But he did not lose his spirit.

He began writing a monthly column from his cell for a magazine in Detroit. It caught my eye. His stuff was as readable as anything in the Detroit papers. Coming from jail, it was especially appealing.

I went to see him but they wouldn't let me in. He was in about for about 3 1/2 years. I told him that before he left the Alabama lockup to take a picture of his cell and blow it up 10 times and hang it on a wall in his house...a reminder of what it was like in there.

Denny made a big comeback in Detroit. He was still bold and brash and that was part of his charm. He became a talk show host on radio and had a TV show with Eli Zaret, a local broadcaster, and the pair opened a restaurant in the suburbs. Again, McLain had it all. And once again, he lost it.

He quit his radio show and lost his TV show, and when the TV went, so did the restaurant. He bought into a meat packing company but the government came down on him, charging he took money from the company's pension fund and used some of it to buy an island off the Atlantic coast.

He was found guilty and sentenced to eight years in prison. He has simply felt the rules do not apply to him—that he could do what he wants, when he wants, to whomever he wants. Too bad, because he was a colorful character and could have had a very good life.

The strange thing is I do not dislike him as others do. I can't explain it either. It is just how I feel.

Chapter 7:
Number 91518 and The Bird

Characters? None was more fascinating than No. 91518.

His name was Jim Kelly and he was a prisoner—a three-time loser—in Jackson (Michigan) Prison. He was editor-in-chief of *The Spectator*, the weekly prison paper. He was a clever guy and I got to know him from getting stuff from him through the mail for my column.

I knew he was special when he said to my readers: "Just a reminder: There are only 11 shoplifting days until Christmas."

I had to visit him and see what this was all about. I went to Jackson Prison three times and we became friends. He was bright, sharp and knowledgeable and—excuse the expression—he did not try to con you. He was in for nonviolent crimes, such as forgery, and knew he deserved his 9½-year term. But he never lost his sense of humor.

This was in the late 1960s. He was just past 30 and sent me some delightful stuff:

- "I won't say the Pittsburgh Steelers are out of the Eastern Division race. All they have to do is win 11 of their last nine games."
- "I gained 20 pounds writing my last column. Every time I came to the end of the line, a bell rang and I had lunch."
- "Don't tell me Jack the Ripper is dead. He works in the prison laundry and does my shirts."
- "Maybe stone walls do not a prison make, but they don't make for a Sheraton Hotel, either."
- "I quit drinking one day and they found me in the gutter. I was just trying to curb my thirst."
- "A friend of mine is stationed in Mississippi and he's so scared down there he won't order a mixed drink."

This happy story had a sad ending. After several years, Kelly was released from prison. He went back to his home in Flint and never spoke to me again. I decided to leave him alone because how could I figure what was in his mind? I wanted to help him if I could but he never made contact with me. He died shortly afterward.

Then there was Pam Eldred, my neighbor. She was not exactly a character. She was Miss America of 1971. She lived around the corner and we never paid much attention to her. In fact, the guys used to call her "pudge" when they saw her in church. She was a quiet lady who entered beauty contests. How could I ever forget the night we were all watching the Miss America pageant on TV from Atlantic City and she wound up as one of the five finalists. Imagine our shock when she won. I mean, Miss America always lived somewhere else, not around the corner.

We were singing and dancing in the family room, even though we really didn't know her. We went over to her house and decorated it with streamers, banners and balloons. After all, she was "our" Miss America.

When she came home, I asked if could take her to lunch at the Press Club. It was always some other guy walking in with the best-looking woman in the place. Now it would be my turn. I told her what I wanted to do and she was terrific. She put on her brightest red dress, which went perfectly with her blond hair, and I could see the looks of envy and hear the mutterings when we walked into the Press Club. I, of course, took her to both newspapers, saying, "I'd like you to meet my neighbor."

What I liked about her was her honesty. When I asked how she could win the Miss America contest, she said: "I've been training for this my entire life. I am a professional contest winner. It gave me an edge over some of the other girls. I knew what to do." I liked that a lot. But how do you study to be beautiful?

Jerry Rideout was an innovative man. He was head of the publicity department for the Buick car company in Flint, Michigan, the man responsible for making the Buick Open a popular golf tournament. He got the idea of putting the players' names on the back of the caddies. When Doug Ford showed up at the Buick Open, it was no problem for Jerry. He just had his people make a sign reading: "Doug Buick."

Jerry worked for *The United Press* during World War II. He didn't know much about sports. He knew very little, in fact. With the regular reporters gone to war, he was asked to cover the Illinois-North-western football game in Evanston. Football was not his specialty.

Buddy Young, the star Illinois running back, scored three times in the first half and Jerry got a message from his office saying if Young scored one more touchdown, he would tie Red Grange's Big Ten record.

He looked at the message and turned to the man sitting next to him and said, "Who the F- is Red Grange?"

The man looked at him and said, "I am."

Howard Cosell may be considered a character. I got along with him pretty well. He came to Detroit for a Monday night football game and I asked what he thought of Lions coach Joe Schmidt. He said, "He couldn't inspire a frog." Poor Schmidt. The label stuck with him for a long time.

Cosell came to town another time to make a speech in Dearborn. I was invited to attend along with my wife. He started in with his familiar comments that sports were corrupt at many levels. He started turning on me. He said it was men like me who were responsible for teams like the New York Giants and Brooklyn Dodgers to leave New York City and seek riches elsewhere. He blamed me for almost everything that was wrong with sports—agents, salaries, greed...the whole magila. I couldn't believe my ears. When it was over, the men who had invited me to dinner came to my table and apologized. I simply said, "I have no idea why he picked on me."

A guy said, "I know why."

We all looked at him.

"I picked him up at the airport and the first thing he asked was: 'Are any sports writers going to be in the audience tonight?' I told him, 'Joe Falls of *The Detroit News*.' He said, 'Good. He will be the target for this evening.'"

Next is Tom Lezouich, a snowmobile driver. I went to Sault Ste. Marie. Michigan, for the 500-mile snowmobile race and he was one of the contestants. They tried to pattern the race after the Indy 500 and all went well until the start of the race. Instead of the expected, "Gentlemen, start your engines," the guy on the public address microphone said, "All right, you guys. Get those things started. And remember—if anything happens to you out there, we're not responsible."

Around and around the sleds went—and the officials became very suspicious. One driver kept coming by with hair blowing from the back of the helmet. One of the officials said: "I think we've got a girl out there." They huddled and decided to bring the sled into the pits. The black flag went out and the sled pulled in and the driver was furious. He asked what was going on. They took him inside their office and told him of their concern.

"I'm no girl," said Tom Lezouich, and pulled down his pants to prove it.

We now come to Jim Bouton, the ex-Yankee pitcher who wrote *Ball Four*, a behind-the-scenes look at his teammates. Some hailed this book as one of great social significance, exposing the players for what they were—calloused and selfish. I thought the book was a disgrace; readable but disgraceful. Bouton had deceived his teammates. They thought he was a teammate when, in fact, he was also playing the role of sports writer. He was able to see things the rest of us could never get near. He violated a privilege. I said all this when Bouton and I were on a TV show together. In fact, I ended one segment by tossing his book over my shoulder and saying I did not want to contaminate myself by even holding it in my lap.

Bouton laughed. He signed a book for me. The inscription read: "To Joe Falls. Maybe you can write a book like this some day . . .when your career is over . . .which should be very soon."

Barry Switzer: You are not supposed to like people just because they treat you well. This is hard to do, and in the case of Switzer, impossible. Michigan was playing Oklahoma in the 1976 Orange Bowl and I went to Norman, Oklahoma, to write about the Sooners' celebrated Wishbone attack. I made arrangements through the Oklahoma publicity man but when I arrived on a Sunday night, who should be at the airport to pick me up but Switzer himself. He took me straight to his house and asked for my wife's name and my home telephone. I gave it to him. He dialed. "Hi, Mary Jane," he said. "This is Barry Switzer and I want you to know that Joe is safe. We've got a drink in his hand, we're going out to get a steak and we've even got him a date. So, sleep well. Bye."

Lou Brock: He was the big player on the St. Louis Cardinals when the Tigers met them in the 1968 World Series. I flew to St. Louis in the final week of the season to get some personal stuff on the players. I found out that Brock owned a florist shop in Clayton, Missouri, and drove out to see him. And there he was, dressed elegantly and smiling, showing me around his place. I said, "Come on,

Lou, what do you know about flowers?" He said, "I know a lot." I said, "Like what?" And he said, "See the ones over there? They're yellow. These are red, and those are purple."

David Justice: My second job, after writing, is working for Special Olympics. A few years ago we held an auction, selling some of the finest stuff that could be gathered. Chuck Daly, coach of the Pistons, was the host and we had uniforms from the likes of Magic Johnson, Michael Jordan, Ted Williams, Joe DiMaggio, Nolan Ryan, Mickey Mantle, Maurice Richard, Gordie Howe and so on. It was a great collection and we made $125,000. But when I sent a bat to Atlanta and asked them to have David Justice sign it for our mentally impaired athletes, he refused. The poor publicity man in Atlanta was very embarrassed when he told me of Justice's refusal. I said, "Did you tell him it was for Special Olympics?" He said, "Yes, but it still didn't matter. He won't sign it." I told the guy to give the bat to some kid at the game and he said: "You don't want it back?" I told him, no, it wouldn't do us any good without his name on it, and I'm sorry to say this, but I do not enjoy any of Justice's success.

Rickey Henderson: I went into the Oakland A's dressing room to get some balls signed for our auction but was a little scared because I'd never asked for autographs before. Reggie Jackson saw my concern and said, "What's wrong?" I told him. He said, "Come on, I'll get them signed for you." He introduced me to Dave Stewart, Jose Canseco, Mark McGwire and they were terrific. They all signed four balls. When I got to Rickey Henderson, he wasn't too interested. I told him they weren't for me but the kids in our program. He said, "How many did the others sign?" I said, "four." He said, "OK, I'll sign three."

I don't get it. A lot of people in my town always want to put down Michael Jordan. I think it's because he came along and ended the Pistons' two-year run on the NBA title. They're dumb. Here we have the greatest player of all time and they don't take the time to appreciate him

When Jordan finished off the Pistons one night in Detroit, I waited until all the media had left and went in to see him. I'd never had any personal contact with him, only from afar. He was sitting there still getting dressed, with a few hangers-on around his locker. The rest of the dressing room was empty.

I went up to him and said, "Michael, see this white hair? I'm too old to b.s. anymore, so you have to listen to me."

He looked up and smiled. He'd probably never heard anything like this and seemed pleased. I did not tell him who I was, only: "I am a Detroit newspaperman and I just wanted to thank you for all the times you spoke to us—both when you won and when you lost. I always appreciated that."

I shook his hand and left.

The next spring, Jordan was trying his hand at baseball. It was a big story. I drove from Lakeland, where the Tigers were training, to Sarasota, where the White Sox were training. I wanted to do my piece on him. When I got there, there was the usual mob outside of the clubhouse—maybe 35 members of the media, some with cameras, some with microphones, some with notebooks. It was a daily scene.

The drive took almost two hours and I had to visit the bathroom. With the clubhouse closed, I thought I would go into the bushes out back. When I went back there, I saw the back door was open. I didn't want to go into the bushes, so I thought I could sneak in and use the men's room, then leave.

When I walked in, the dressing room was empty. Only one player was in there—outfielder Michael Jordan. He saw me and called out, "Hey, Falls, get over here!"

I was more than surprised.

I walked over and he said: "What do you need?"

I said, "You know what I need."

He gave me a half hour, just as Joe D. had done, and I left feeling very good.

Finally, we give you Bobby Knight, who is something of a fraud. He would like you to believe he is on the outs with the sports writers of America, especially after he let writer John Feinstein into his inner circle and Feinstein held him up for ridicule in his book, *On the Brink*.

The truth is, Knight has favorites all through my business—myself included.

My first encounter with him was at the NCAA finals in Philadelphia in 1976. That's when he threw a fan into a garbage can and I landed on him for being such a low-life. His team won the title and I wrote another piece saying the Hoosiers were one of the most disciplined basketball teams I had ever seen.

Knight sent me a letter.

It said, "I read both of your columns. The first one went into the trash can. I am making copies of the second one and using it a recruiting tool. Thank you for your interest."

How can you ignore this man? I once asked him about smoking. He said, "It's simple. You are not allowed to smoke in my car, my home or my office. I burp but I don't burp in public."

The last time I went to see Knight, he was throwing people out of practice in the gym in Bloomington, Indiana. I was sitting there when some guy with a clipboard came around and asked my name, my place of business and my reason for being there. He did this with everyone who was watching, maybe a dozen in all. He took the clipboard down to Knight, who looked at the names and started making notations on the paper. That's when some were asked to leave. I was allowed to stay. I interviewed Knight after practice and, as always, he was marvelous. He likes to fish and I asked him where was his best fishing hole. He said, "It's in Montana, but I ain't saying where because I don't want you Eastern guys messing it up."

My most memorable characters, however, have been on the Tigers.

Take Bill Faul. He was a pitcher in the early 1960s. He thought he was a hypnotist. He felt he could hypnotize the batters, or himself, and I never believed it until one day I walked past his room at the Holiday Inn in Lakeland. A young girl was sitting in the doorway and he had his car pulled up on the sidewalk, with one tire on the sidewalk and the other in the parking lot. He had turned on his directional signal. He was trying to hypnotize her with the blinking light.

And then there was Dave Rozema, another pitcher, who was the resident flake in Detroit for a long time. I never thought much of it until the Sunday in spring training when he decided to wash his new car, using Brillo soap pads.

Sandy Amoros was an outfielder who came over from the Brooklyn Dodgers. He told everyone his name sounded like "love on the beach."

Steve Bilko, the massive first basemen, knew he had to lose weight, so he took "steamers" in his hotel room, stuffing towels under the door of the bathroom and around the windows and turning on all the hot water faucets.

Gates Brown, the pinch-hitting star, would go out to banquets and when he was asked what his buddy, Willie Horton, took in school, he would say, "Willie took algebra, English, history and overcoats."

Ike Brown, a happy-go-lucky guy, told everyone he was the Tigers' DS—designated sitter.

Pete Burnside, the skinny pitcher, ran for hours and hours in spring training, prompting manager Jimmy Dykes to say, "If you win games with your legs, this guy would be a 30-game winner."

Norm Cash was so frustrated when Nolan Ryan was pitching a no-hitter against the Tigers that he took a table leg to the plate with him, telling the umpire, "I may as well try it with this—my bat isn't working."

Pitcher Dave Boswell got into a fight with Billy Martin in an alley behind a bar in Detroit and was beaten up. He told everyone: "This time he was the pitcher and I was the catcher." Paul Foytack, the quick-witted pitcher, was asked for his reaction when the Tigers were screening in the lower deck in rightfield to cut down on homers and said, "What about the upper deck?"

Outfielder Johnny Groth lived in Chicago with his wife and five daughters but would stay at the team's hotel when the Tigers played in Chicago, explaining, "Hey, I've got to get my rest." Outfielder Willie Horton hit a high foul in Fenway Park and backed away in horror when the ball struck a pigeon and the pigeon fell dead on home plate.

Outfielder Charley Maxwell liked to needle the sports writers, saying, "I used to work on a Tri-Weekly in Paw Paw. We'd try to get it out weekly." Infielder Stan Papi asked the sports writers not to print his salary: "It's so small, I'm ashamed of it."

Infielder Ron Samford once swung at Hoyt Wilhelm's knuckleball after the bat fell from his hands. Rusty Staub insisted they put a clause in his contract saying runways had to be a certain length before he would get on any planes with the Tigers.

Then there was Mark Fidrych, "The Bird."

You could never get near his locker. Cakes and flowers and presents and boxes of mail were stacked around him. You had to climb over them to get close to The Bird.

The fans loved him more than any athlete in Detroit. And how long did he last? One summer. One fleeting summer. For four months —June, July, August and September of 1976—he flashed across our sky. He won 19 games and lost only nine. But no one talked about his record. They spoke of his style. His spirit. His enthusiasm.

He talked to the ball: "Come on, ball. Stay low, stay low. Hit the corner." He smoothed the mound with his hand and talked to his fielders, waving to them when they made a good play. He waved to the fans, and they waved back.

Detroit was in an economic crisis, with the Japanese putting heavy pressure on our auto makers. The city was struggling in a kind of depression.

The Bird made everyone feel better.

He gave them joy. He gave them pleasure. He gave them a reason to forget their troubles.

His base pay was $16,000 but he earned millions for the Tigers. He became the single greatest attraction this team had ever known—greater, even, than Denny McLain in the year he won his 31 games.

And then, the next spring, it all ended.

Fidrych came to camp and was as nervous as—well, a bird. He was flying all over the place, trying to get everyone's attention. He was jumping over fences, racing around the field, making all kinds of noises, crazy gestures, and acting a little looney. He was trying to tell everyone he was back and all was OK: "Hey, world, look at me. It's me! I'm here and everything is wonderful!"

When I saw these crazy antics, I told Doug Mintline of *The Flint Journal:* "If he doesn't tone down, he's going to hurt himself." I wrote this in my paper.

I saw him slip when he tried to vault over a pile of bats one day and thought that was it. His injury happened while he was shagging flies. Someone knocked a ball into the outfield. Fidrych had no play and should have let it go but he lunged for the ball and when he landed, his knee gave away under him. Nobody knew it, but that was the end of his career.

He tried to come back many times but made the mistake of favoring the knee, which caused damage to his shoulder.

I will never forget the press conference they called at his hospital after the season began. The room was packed with doctors and nurses (lots of nurses) as well as writers, broadcasters, cameramen and photographers.

When Fidrych saw me, he pointed at me and started crying. He said, "There's the man who wanted me to get hurt. That's him, over by the wall."

I was stunned. I couldn't believe he got it so wrong. All I wrote is that he could get hurt if he didn't calm down. The doctors and nurses looked at me as if I had some kind of disease. I'll never forget the expressions on the faces of those nurses.

I didn't say anything. How could I explain, in that moment, what really had happened? They wouldn't have understood it. It would have sounded like I was trying to alibi my way out of the situation. So, I remained silent...with a chill running through my body.

As they wheeled Fidrych from the room, a rival writer leaned over to Fidrych and whispered, "Read my column, Mark. *I* never write anything bad about you."

Welcome to the wonderful world of journalism.

As the years passed, Fidrych matured. I went to see him at his farm in Massachusetts. He was very cordial. I figured all the pressures on him were too much to handle. I wrote a piece saying he was more of a man after baseball than he was in baseball, and I think he liked it.

Chapter 8:
Madness at Munich

My Olympic experience has been rather checkered. Happy and sad. I've covered seven Olympics—three summer and four winter. I like winter better because I like the figure skating. Never thought I'd ever say such a thing. The sport fascinates me, not so much because of its beauty but because it demands so much of the skaters. They have to be all but perfect. They simply cannot make a mistake, and I've seen some of the greatest skaters in the world flop on the ice or wobble on their skates. I hold my breath hoping it doesn't happen, but it does, and I feel bad for them because they can't go back and undo it. Sometimes, a lifetime of practice can be wiped out in a few moments. I know of no other sport that asks more of its competitors.

Mexico City was my first Olympics in 1968. I got there late, a few days after the Games started, because I was in St. Louis covering the Tigers in the World Series. When I showed up at the press center in Mexico City, they never heard of me. They spent the better part of a day figuring out what to do with me, until finally they gave me a mattress and told me to follow that man over there and he would take me to my dwelling. He didn't speak English, so I just followed him.

He took me to a gleaming apartment building, obviously just built for the Olympics, and we rode up to the sixth floor on an elevator. He opened the door to an apartment and pointed to the kitchen floor. This is where I would live for nearly three weeks. I couldn't complain because he could not understand me, so I gave him a tip in American money, and he smiled, tipped his hat and left. I threw the mattress on the floor and looked around the apartment. It had three bedrooms and somebody was living in them. I didn't know who yet, since I assumed they were all out covering the Games.

I looked into the living room. It had no furniture, only a wooden table which held a massive jug of water. I assumed that's what we were drinking—not the Mexican water. How well I knew this lesson. I had covered the major league baseball meetings in Mexico City a few years earlier and came home with a case of the galloping gout. My foot hurt so much that I could not touch it and did not want anyone to even look at it. It felt as if my toes had been blown off by a shotgun.

Now here I was, back in Mexico City, and I looked at the jug of water with grave concern.

The bad part were the bathrooms. They had two of these and they were nicely appointed—bright lights and fancy tile. One thing was missing. The floor. They hadn't gotten to putting down the tile yet and both bathrooms had dirt floors. It turned out I was staying with seven or eight other guys, all friendly, all foreign, and all we could do was smile at each other. In no time at all, we were kicking the dirt out of the bathroom, into the hallways, and all around the apartment. Nobody ever came to clean it up and nobody thought to buy a broom and dust pail. Pretty soon, the dirt found its way into my abode in the kitchen. I tried to brush it away with my socks, but that didn't work so well. Within a week, I was suffering from a severe case of Montezuma's Revenge, as well as another spectacular case of the gout, and I left Mexico City in a broken condition, never thinking I could make it home.

I was in the stadium the day Bob Beamon set his record long jump but I did not see it since I could not hold my head up. This was not the greatest experience of my life.

The next one, in Munich, was even worse. In fact, it was my worst experience as a newspaperman. It was 1972 and the weather and the games were glorious. I was enjoying everything, especially the weiner schnitzel at a German restaurant with the other guys at three o'clock in the afternoon. We ate there every day, weiner schnitzel and German beer. I couldn't handle the beer and had to take a nap before writing. I could do this because of the seven-hour time break back to Detroit.

I was in a nice apartment, along with Joe McGuff, who wrote for the *Kansas City Star.* We got along well because we were baseball writers and had a lot in common. One day we decided to visit Dachau, the German concentration camp. It was just outside of town. We went with another writer from Louisiana whose name I can't remember. A taxi took us there, about 15 minutes away, and this is the truth: The moment I got out of the cab, I said to Joe: "You smell that?" It was a foul odor, one that made me wretch. I'm sure it was my imagination but the odor seemed very real. Joe smelled it, too. We saw the ovens and gas chambers. I picked up a stone from the courtyard and told myself I would keep it in my home forever as a reminder of what had transpired here, hoping it would never happen again. That stone still sits on a shelf in our living room.

A little later, I was watching TV in the afternoon when it showed a woman sitting up in bed with bare breasts. I nearly fell on the floor. I had never seen anything like this on our TV stations. There she was, looking luscious and lovely, and some guy was standing in the door of the room holding an attache case.

He held it up and said something in German. The subtitle under the picture said, "This is an attache case."

He said something else in German. The subtitle read, "This is my attache case."

Quite clearly, this was a language program for visitors from other countries. But why a half-naked woman, I didn't know. I called Joe into the room and said, "Look at this, will you?" I wanted proof I had actually seen such a thing. I did not want to be accused of making it up when I told the story back home. Joe took one look at the picture and said, "I'll be damned."

I guess we were still in an age of innocence.

My boss at *The Free Press* was Kurt Luedtke, the executive editor. He was the man who won an Academy Award for writing the screenplay to "Out of Africa." More on this in a moment.

He called one day and said, "How about a column on America's sweetheart?"

I said, "Who's that?" I don't think he liked my answer.

"Olga Korbut, the Russian gymnast," he said. "It would be nice if you wrote something about her. Everyone is talking about her."

I tried to explain this was all but impossible to do but I don't think he liked hearing that, either. The International Olympic Committee gave only one press credential a day to the American press delegation for gymnastics and it was never going to get down to me. I'd put my name on the list but I knew The AP, UPI, *New York Times, Washington Post*—the heavy hitters—would go ahead of me. I told him I would do my best but I never got into the gymnastics, even though I went to the press office every day and asked how my request was coming along.

This was nothing compared to what was to follow.

Luedtke called again, in the middle of the final week, and told me to come home. He said, "We can sell more newspapers on you writing baseball than covering the Olympics." The Tigers were in the race for the Eastern Division title. This was the first week of September, which meant nothing was going to be decided, but when your boss tells you to come home, you go home.

I told him that I'd been in Munich long enough and that I didn't want to stay anymore, either, but three big events were coming up: Jim Ryun, the great American miler, going up against Kenya's fabled Kip Keino in the 1,500 meters, the Americans playing the Russians in the basketball finals (where the Russians were allowed to throw the ball in three times in the final moments to finally win the game) and a doping scandal was just breaking on the U.S. swimming team.

"Don't argue with me," Luedtke said. "Come home!"

The next morning, at 6 a.m., I left my apartment building in the Olympic complex. I walked past the apartment next door where several of the Israeli athletes already had been killed and summoned a cab and told him to take me to the airport. He was playing the radio—American music—so I did not hear any news, though I could not have understood it anyway.

When I checked in at the airport, they took me into a small room where my bags were thoroughly searched while two soldiers holding sub-machine guns pointed toward the ceiling watched the proceeding.

On the plane, I asked the stewardess if that was how they always checked the baggage.

She said, "That's because of the spectator killed in the Olympic Stadium last night."

To understand journalism, you must know that when a truly big story breaks, the information sometimes leaks out in dribs and drabs, some of it incorrect. That's what happened this time. Something terrible had happened but nobody had the facts. Somebody had spread the story of a fan being killed but it was erroneous. When we landed in London, I bought all the British papers—nearly 10 of them—but saw nothing about any killing in Munich.

I got on another plane and flew across the ocean to Detroit, arriving about 3 o'clock in the afternoon. My wife was there to meet me and she had an awful look on her face.

"I was hoping you wouldn't be here," she said.

I said, "What do you mean by that?"

"You don't know what happened, do you?" she said.

"What happened?"

She said we'd better sit on the bench over in the corner. She was holding a late-afternoon copy of *The Detroit News* and had it folded up.

"This is what happened," she said.

She opened the paper and an eight-column headline screamed out at me. It said Israeli athletes had been assassinated at the Olympics.

And there, on page one, was a picture of the building where they lived—the building I had walked in front of that morning.

Talk about trying to get hold of yourself...I simply could not believe what I was seeing. My wife looked at me and now I could see the sadness in her face.

"What'll I do?"

She said, "I'd report to work. See what's going on there."

We drove downtown and I have to say my mind wasn't very clear. It was spinning. Munich. Murder. Israelis. Terrorists.

In the nearly three weeks I was there, I became sensitive to the security. I knew the Germans were on the spot. If they had too much security, it could be said they were still a military state since this was only 25 years since the end of the war. Too little security and they could be second-guessed for not taking the proper precautions against any terrorism. Frankly, I felt sorry for them because it seemed like a no-win situation.

When I took the elevator to the newsroom floor of the *Free Press*, Neil Shine, who was Luedtke's assistant, was standing there. He took one look at me and acted as if he had seen a ghost.

"What...are...you...doing...here?" he mumbled.

"Kurt told me to come home."

Shine had a stunned look on his face. He told me they had just talked about me in their regular newsroom meeting. They had me down to write all kinds of stuff from Munich, page one, the back page, the sports page, my column. And now, here I was, standing in an elevator on the newsroom floor.

This is where I made a mistake.

I went over to Luedtke's office, which was at the end of the room, behind some glass partitions. I saw him sitting at his desk, looking down at some papers before him. I told his secretary, who was sitting outside the office: "Would you tell Mr. Luedtke I am here." He never looked up, and my life at *The Free Press* was never the same again.

I guess I should have protected him and thought up some kind of story why I was back. But, I was mad. I knew a tremendous story when I saw one and felt awful I could not do a thing about it. We used typewriters in those days and I wrote a baseball column on the way home on the plane. I started out: "Hang on, Billy Martin. I'm coming home to help you."

My wife and I drove home. She was silent and I was in a funk.

She said, "You can't let that baseball column stand. You can't let your office down. You've got to write one more column about the Olympics."

I won't repeat what I said to her. It wasn't nice, nor was it intended to be. I told her what my office could do.

I sat there into the evening watching this awful news from Munich. Chris Schenkel was doing the main reporting but (as we found out later) it got to be too much for him and ABC-TV brought in Jim McKay to take his place. I kept feeling lower and lower, saying to myself I should be there and writing these things myself.

My wife kept pressing me to substitute my column. Our deadline was 11 p.m., so I had plenty of time to do it.

I said, "They want baseball, they've got baseball."

Sometime around nine o'clock (the time gets fuzzy) here was Jim McKay, with that terrible look on his face, saying, "They're gone. They're all gone." The rest of the Israeli team had been killed as the terrorists tried to escape at the airport. The terrorists were killed, too. It was too much to believe.

My wife said, "Do it. Change your column."

She was right. If Jim McKay could do his job, I could do my job. I could not put my own feelings ahead of my newspaper's needs. I went into the den and wrote my reaction to the massacre. I did not use a Munich dateline but started out by saying: "Don't stop these Games. Don't give into the bums. If you do that, they win, and they should never be allowed to win."

The column ran in its regular place the next day, and while I did hear from Mr. Luedtke, I felt a little better about myself.

Red Smith wrote they should stop the Olympics. He said this tragedy was far greater than any sports event. He said they should be halted out of respect for the slain Israelis.

I wondered if I'd written the wrong thing, but this thought lasted about three seconds. I knew I was right—and still do. You never give in to the terrorists, no matter what the cost.

My days at *The Free Press* got very dark.

I did not know how upset Luedtke was over the Munich incident. For the next five years, he did not give me a penny raise, and here I was his No. 1 sports columnist, producing all the time for him. Neil Shine went behind his back and got me two $2,000 raises, pushing my salary from $30,000 to $34,000. I was involved in a divorce and was hurting for money. It didn't matter to Luedtke. He was not going to raise my pay under any circumstances.

He took away my title of sports editor and reduced my assignments until I almost never went out of town to work. He knew I loved to write and the final straw was when he drew up a new schedule and had me writing only three times a week, with four days off. What did I need with four days off?

I went to *The Detroit News* and asked them for a job. Bill Giles, the executive editor and second best boss I ever had, hired me for $40,000, a six-thousand dollar raise. Some people called me a mercenary. *Detroit Monthly Magazine* wrote that my new salary was $80,000. My wife was furious. She didn't understand how they could write such an untruth. I told her to forget it. That's the way it goes in this business. They don't always check the facts.

The day I told *The Free Press* I was leaving, the Yankees and Red Sox were playing for the American League pennant in a one-game playoff in Fenway Park. I was not allowed to be there, so I wrote it from a distance, just as I had done with my Olympic column, and said to myself: "This is why I have to leave. He is not letting me do my job."

Shine and others at the paper were shocked at my decision. They knew what I was up against, but couldn't do anything about it. Leudtke was too strong. Shine asked me to stay but I told him I couldn't do that because I would be breaking my word to *The News,* and once I broke my word, my word would be no good.

He said, "Will you just stay in a room for a few hours? Something is happening and I'll get back to you very soon."

I liked Neil. He was a fair guy. I figured I could do that much for him. But no way was I going to stay.

He came back and said: "OK, something will happen tomorrow. Just go home and don't talk to anyone."

What was happening is that Luedtke was being fired. He had lost other talented people, all leaving because they did not like working for him, and I must have been the proverbial straw. Jim Batten, a top executive of the Knight-Ridder chain in Miami, figured enough was enough and decided to let Luedtke go. The next day, Luedtke announced his resignation and I was told that when the workers in the newsroom saw the announcement on the bulletin board, they stood up and gave out with a rousing ovation.

Charley Vincent, a writer in the sports department, said later: "You died for our sins, but not soon enough."

In any case, Luedtke, a brilliant man with an unfortunate mean streak, went on to write "Absence of Malice," a popular movie based on the newspaper business. He followed with his award-winning script for "Out of Africa." I guess it all came out even: I got away from him and he got a chance to become rich and famous.

My next Olympic assignment was the Summer Games in Montreal in 1976. That's where I had the privilege of sitting in the Montreal Forum one afternoon and watching Nadia Comenici record her perfect 10 in gymnastics. What I remember best was where I lived.

They put us in dorms at the University de Montreal—an apartment house much like the one in Mexico City, but older. What they didn't tell us is that some of the students hung around in the summertime.

I was just coming out of the shower the first morning when I blundered into one student who was washing her teeth at the sink.

I had nothing on. She wore a dress and a smile.

"Bon jour," she said, walking out of the room.

I said, "And bon jour to you!"

In 1980, it was the Winter Games in Lake Placid. Winter Games? There was almost no snow in the streets, mostly slush. I was impressed that they had snow at all the venues and the competition went on without a hitch. I knew nothing about speedskating but was taken by Eric Heiden winning all those gold medals. We watched from a window of a high school which served as press headquarters for the skaters, and the man took my breath away. You could see he was the best, but he had to do it, and he did. I wound up writing all kinds of stories about speed skating.

The big moment was when the U.S. hockey team beat the Russians. It happened on a Friday night. The Russians dominated the game from start to finish, launching something like 65 shots at the American net, but ultimately losing 4-3. I left with the crowd and it was a Cinderella scene—a soft snow falling in the picturesque village and everyone smiling and singing and hugging each other. I wish I could have shared the moment with them but I had to hustle back to the press center to get my column written. The pressure got to me and I didn't write a very good column. It was very forced, not what my newspaper needed.

In 1984, it was Sarajevo, the most memorable of all the Olympics, and you can only imagine how I felt when I met the loveliest people on this earth and then saw their city shelled and torn apart in the war.

These people were precious. Tom Callahan, who wrote for the *Washington Post,* called them "black and white television people from the 1940s." It was not a criticism but a commentary on how far they were behind us. They came from a much simpler time. They did not have the problems which existed in our country: crime, drugs, killings. They were poor people, poor but sweet.

When the U.S. press delegation arrived, they were given tours of the city. One group saw a woman hanging clothes in her backyard, her very muddy backyard. She was dressed in a bland smock. When she saw these visitors looking at her from afar, she raced into her house. She returned in a few moments wearing a bright dress, pretty shoes, and she had a flower in her hair. She went about her business of hanging the laundry.

Women played a big role at the press center. These were housewives who were called in to run the teletype machines. The husbands worked at their jobs and could not be there.

One of these women took a liking to me. I cannot spell her name—it sounded like Bill-YAN-Ah—and she was wonderful. She was a small, round woman (5X5) and would do my laundry, no small consideration since I couldn't get it done anywhere else. She'd come by my work place every day with a complete complement of medicines. The Americans suffered from "Yugo-Throat," a malady caused by the heavy smog in Sarajevo. We all got it to one degree or another. The guys would come by each morning and take what they needed. They never knew who put it there, or asked.

Bill-YAN-ah was married to a school teacher and had two children. In time, I met her family. They all seemed so shy.

They did not have any entertainment in the restaurants, so the families would get up and sing. First, the father. Then, the mother. Then the children. You can imagine how warm that felt.

I wanted to see the spot where the Arch Duke Ferdinand was assassinated—the incident that started World War I. I left the Press Center and hailed a cab. It was a yellow car and when the driver saw me waving, he pulled up. I jumped into the back seat and told him where I wanted to go. He saluted and away we went. It wasn't far. Five minutes away, down some river, across a bridge, and there we were, at the exact spot of the shooting.

I offered him some Dinars, which was local currency, but he waved me off. I didn't know what to do, so I offered him my hand. He shook it, smiled, and saluted again.

As I got out of the back seat, I looked at the roof of the car to see what kind of cab I was in. I mean, no charge. A smile, a handshake, a salute.

There was nothing on the roof. Then, it hit me. I wasn't in a taxi at all; I had jumped into somebody's private car and he took me to where I wanted to go. As he drove away, I tried to call to him, to say thank you again, but he was gone. I thought to myself: "If this was Detroit, he would have taken me to see Jimmy Hoffa."

One night two AP photographers were finished with their work and wanted to play cards. It was late. On the way home, they asked their cab driver where they might buy some playing cards. He understood and took them to two stores, neither of which had playing cards. They decided to go home, it was too late, anyway. The driver took them there and the photographers said goodnight.

A half hour later, there was a tapping on the door of their room. It was the cab driver. He was bowing and holding out a frayed deck of cards he had gotten from his home. The two photographers looked at him, smiling but a little dumbfounded.

The Press Center was located in a large basement of a shopping center. Each day, a young girl of about 18, dressed in a pretty outfit, would come by and ask each writer what he would like to drink. After two or three days, she knew what everyone wanted. She would simply come by your desk, bow, and give you your favorite soft drink. I met her and her boyfriend the day after the Olympics. I was finishing up my last story when they came by to say hello.

I stood up and said to the boy: "For three weeks, your lady has been bowing to us and bringing us soft drinks. If you don't mind, I would like to return the favor."

I bowed to her.

She smiled. I smiled. The boy smiled.

The final night was the most memorable of all. That's when we saw all the husbands and all the children. They formed a ring around the floor of the Press Center and, holding hands and swaying back and forth, serenaded us for more than an hour. We all stopped writing, a few of us started crying.

These were the people who were slaughtered by those bombs. I often thought of Bill-YAN-ah and her family. I hope she is well, but do not know.

Calgary in 1988 was memorable because it was so warm. The Chinook winds were blowing and the temperatures rose to some surprising heights. There was absolutely no snow in the city. They had put down tons of sand when the snow was there but now that the snow had melted all that was left was the sand. This blew around fiercely in the winds. It would crinkle against your eyeglasses and rattle against your teeth. You learned to keep your mouth closed, not an easy thing for sports writers.

My wife was waiting for me at the Tigers' camp in Lakeland, Florida. When we talked on the phone, we compared temperatures. More often than not, it was warmer in Calgary than in Florida.

Finally, there was Albertville in 1992. What I remember most was my room. It was so narrow I could touch both walls with the palm of my hands. It felt like a jail cell, just wonderful for one who is afflicted with claustrophobia. The people were pleasant, so that helped. All you had to do was get past Igor, a ferocious sounding guard dog, as you walked up the hill to the hotel each night.

I learned to say "Nice Igor" in French.

Chapter 9:
18 Managers

Baseball managers are more fun than football coaches. You can sit around and chat with them. You can do it in their offices, on the bench or out by the batting cage. Very nice, very relaxed. A good way to do your job.

Football coaches are usually on the field, in meetings or watching films. You seldom see them, except under controlled circumstances. Usually at a press conference, where the TV cameras are rolling, and what's the sense of asking questions because TV will use the answers that night and your newspaper doesn't come out until the next day? This is why I never go to the Super Bowl, or haven't in over 15 years. Too many media people around. It is called "herd journalism" and that's exactly what it is. We're like a herd of cattle being moved from one location to another, never getting a chance to get close to the participants in the game. And they're always giving you food to offset the fact you can't get any personal stuff for your stories. At one Super Bowl, they fed us four times a day as we went from the press hotel to one camp to the other camp and back to the hotel.

Let me tell you about Joe Namath. It was Super Bowl III—the one where he guaranteed victory for the New York Jets, and delivered. The Jets were staying in Fort Lauderdale and they'd haul the press up there each day from Miami. The way it worked was the Jets would have a meeting in the morning, meet the media at lunchtime, then work out in the afternoon.

This one day Namath was giving a special interview to some of his favorite writers, mostly from New York. It was at poolside of the hotel. They were talking in a group next to where I was sitting on a beach chair. I could hear what was being said and couldn't help myself. I leaned over and asked a question. It was the wrong thing to do. Namath looked at me like he was smelling something bad. How dare I be so rude? I didn't think I had done anything wrong but obviously I had made a grave mistake. I had broken into his private world.

If that wasn't bad enough, I soon realized I was sitting on something bumpy. It was Namath's playbook. You can imagine the look he got when he found out that such treasured piece of information was covered by my butt.

One of the great journalistic scenes of modern times took place when the Jets, with Namath at the controls, played the New York Giants in an exhibition game at the Yale Bowl in New Haven. I went there for the game, thinking it was an historic occasion, and again Namath was not very cooperative. He was not available after the game. But did that deter Sid Hartman of the *Minneapolis Tribune?* It did not. Sid was a columnist for his paper and also did a radio show on the side. It seemed as if he spent more time talking to people with his faithful tape recorder than writing his column. He had flown half the country for this moment and when Namath went into the shower, Sid went with him, holding his faithful tape recorder. While the rest of us looked on in disbelief, Namath allowed Sid to interview him while both got soaking wet from the water. I had never seen such dedication in my life, but Sid got what he wanted, while the rest of us went away, grumbling.

I covered Super Bowl I in Los Angeles. In fact, I was the first writer on the scene. I got there 10 days ahead of the game. Why, I don't know. I guess I was little caught up in what I was doing. It was Green Bay of the NFL against Kansas City of the AFL, and I checked in at the Kansas City camp in Long Beach. Hank Stram, the KC coach, felt a little sorry for me since I was all by myself. He gave me all kinds of time, and this relationship has lasted until this day.

One of the KC players was Fred Arbanas, a tight end who had played at Michigan State. A perfect story for me. I went to his room and did an interview. Ed Budde, the big lineman, was sitting up in bed listening to what was going on. He never said a word, just kind of glared at me. He, too, had played at Michigan State and maybe he was mad I wasn't interviewing him. Arbanas had only one good eye, so I felt he was the story.

When we were finished, Arbanas asked me who I was picking in the game.

I told him Green Bay. Everybody was picking Green Bay but when I uttered those two words, Budde sat up in bed and his look turned to steel.

"What score you picking?" said Arbanas.

"Green Bay 35, Kansas City 10."

With that, Budde leaped from the bed and went after me. Arbanas was quick, thank heaven. He blocked his way, holding him off and saying, "I think you'd better get out of here."

I set the American Indoor Record for Leaving Hotel Rooms— two seconds flat, and I didn't go back. The final score was Green Bay 35, Kansas City 10, and I've always wondered if Budde remembered my prediction.

All this Super Bowl stuff was new, and so the morning of the game, Jim Taylor, our pro football writer at *The Free Press,* thought it would be a nice touch if we left a note in commissioner Pete Rozelle's mail box wishing him a "Happy Super Sunday." Never heard from him, either.

Some of the guys drove up to the Green Bay camp in Santa Barbara, hoping to get something to write from the Packers. Coach Vince Lombardi wouldn't see us.

We were having some drinks in the hotel bar when word came down he had no time for newspapermen. A wasted day. Everyone was complaining, threatening to write some nasty stuff about The Great Man. I had a better idea. When the check came—for about $72 —I signed Vince Lombardi's name, and we left. Again, I never heard any more.

If you must know, I liked Vince Lombardi. Or, rather, I liked his teams. It was fascinating the way the Green Bay Packers played in the 1960s. They were the ultimate team—strong on offense, strong on defense. Not dazzling, just strong. If you didn't like that sweep with Jim Taylor carrying the ball and the pulling guards blocking, football was not your game.

I got into it one time with Lombardi. It was after a game in Milwaukee. The Lions had played the Packers and we were waiting for The Great Man to come out and talk to us. About 12 of us were huddled in a hallway outside the Green Bay dressing room.

I don't recall if the Packers or Lions won the game but Lombardi was not in a good mood when he showed up. Jerry Green of *The Detroit News* asked him something and Lombardi got all over him. He was giving it to Jerry pretty good, while the rest of us just looked on.

I felt embarrassed and finally said to Lombardi: '"Hey, he didn't do anything wrong. He just asked you a question. We don't know as much football as you do. If you don't want to answer it, fine. But you have no right to talk to him this way. We don't talk to you that way."

Lombardi stopped in mid-sentence. He looked at me. To his credit, he shook his head as if to understand what I said. He didn't apologize to Jerry but was cooperative the rest of the way.

My son Bob loved Lombardi. He was growing up at a time when the Packers were great. On the day Lombardi died of cancer, I had to pick Bobby up at school. I told him what had happened and he sat there in the front seat of the car and was silent all the way home.

As we were pulling into the driveway, I could see the tears running down his face.

He said, "I didn't think rocks died."

I had the lead on my column that day.

Getting back to baseball managers, the most fascinating manager I knew was Casey Stengel. You could not get enough of him. He would sit in the dugout before the games and talk for what seemed like hours. You never asked him a question. You didn't have to. Somebody would say it was a nice day, and he was off. You never really understood what he was saying, but it didn't matter. He was simply delightful. You told yourself if you listened long enough, it all made sense. I'm not sure that's right. It was just great entertainment. At first, I started taking notes, then I realized my notes didn't make sense, so I'd just listen.

One day, in Detroit, the Tigers beat the Yankees in 10 innings when Earl Torgeson stole home against pitcher Bob Turley. We all went to the Yankee dressing room to get some comments from Stengel. They kept the door closed and by the time it was open, Stengel was gone. The other writers left, muttering as we always do when things don't go our way. I thought I would be a good newspaperman and go downtown to the Yankees' hotel and look for Stengel.

When I walked into the lobby, he was buying something at the cigar stand.

I excused myself, told him who I was, and wondered how he felt about Torgeson stealing home.

He said, "Why don't you go out to the stadium and ask Mr. Turley. He's still winding up."

The best manager was Leo Durocher, but I never got to know him. He was before my time. I always felt he had more influence on a game than another other manager. He could literally will his players to victory.

I tried to interview him once in later years—when he managed the Chicago Cubs—but he knocked me off. I still think of him as No. 1.

Another uneasy moment took place at the training camps in Arizona. I've been there only once but felt I had to do it in order to have a full understanding of how baseball worked. I went to see Frank Robinson, who, as I recall, was managing the San Francisco Giants. I'd always had great respect for him. He was one of the toughest hitters of my time, along with Jackie Robinson and Yogi Berra, a great clutch hitter.

Robinson was standing along the leftfield foul line yukking it up with some friends while his team was working out. I approached him, introduced myself, and he kept right on talking, as if I didn't exist.

I didn't know what to do. I knew he'd heard me—certainly he saw me—but I wasn't there as far as he was concerned. I felt foolish and didn't know what to say or do, so I said nothing and just stood there.

He'd turn to me every few minutes and say something like, "So you're a big baseball writer, eh?"

His friends would chuckle with each of these biting comments and then it hit me what was going on. He was going to show off for them by putting me down.

But a strange thing happened. The longer I stood there, his friends began realizing who I was—a legitimate reporter trying to get a story—and, one by one, they stopped laughing at Robinson's comments.

Then Robinson started picking up on it and he said, "So, tell me, who do you write your great stories for?" I said, *"The Detroit News* and *The Sporting News."*

His expression changed. So did his voice. So did his comments. He started in with, "Hey, Joe, it's good to have you here. How can I help you?"

By the time we walked off the field, Robinson had his arm around my shoulder and couldn't do enough for me. I wondered why he had to go through this whole bit and, as the years passed and I dwelled on this moment, I realized he did it because he was Frank Robinson, nothing more, nothing less, and this is how he did things.

It was pretty sad.

The best manager I knew was Al Lopez, the Señor who managed and won at Cleveland, then managed and won with the Chicago White Sox. He had a way with pitchers, getting the most out of them. I figured this came from all those years as a catcher in the National League. I was told he had a nasty streak when he got mad, so I made it a point never to get him mad.

I've had 18 managers in Detroit. Sparky Anderson was the best, personally and professionally. Some others were interesting in their own way.

Fred Hutchinson was first. He was a bear of a man and I was intimidated by the hair on his chest when he took off his uniform shirt and talked to us in his office after the games. This was the reaction of a rookie writer. Hutch was a good guy, really soft under his bold exterior. He was good to the press. We'd heard stories of how mad he'd get when he was a pitcher with the Tigers, storming off the mound and breaking all the light bulbs in the tunnel leading back to the dressing room. He would break up the furniture in the club-house, then walk all the way to his home in Grosse Pointe, 10 or 15 miles away. I hoped I would see this side of the man because it would make good reading, but never did. He simply answered our questions. I never saw him get angry.

Bucky Harris was all but finished as a manager when the Tigers brought him in to replace Hutchinson in 1956. Owner Spike Briggs did it because he liked Harris. He remembered him from his boy-hood growing up around the ball park and brought him back be-cause he was a favorite. Bucky was 59 and showed it. He had lost much of his interest in the game, but a payday was a payday, and he took the job in Detroit, knowing he would not get any heat from the top. He was starting to fail physically. His hands would shake so that it was difficult for him to write out his lineups. Even more difficult was trying to drink beer after the games. He would have to lean over and put his lips to the cup to steady himself, then raise the cup to his mouth. Not a pleasant scene, but we got used to it. I felt bad for him but couldn't do anything about it. You could ask Harris questions but you knew he didn't like answering them. I always got the idea he had been asked these things many times before and was tired of the whole process. He lasted two seasons.

Jack Tighe was next and if you didn't like this man, you didn't like anyone. I never knew a finer person in baseball, and it was sad to realize that he was in over his head, and lasted less than a year and a half. He came out of the minors and enjoyed life and everyone around him. He made everyone feel good, but the team was so short of talent that all his efforts—all his Irish humor—could not help.

One day we were sitting on the bench at the Tigers' early-early camp in Lakeland. We called it that because they brought in a lot of kids in the first week of February, hoping to find some who might help. It was hot and you could hear the grasshoppers making noises in the grass. A squad game was dragging along and everyone was bored when I asked head scout Ed Katalinas: "Ed, let's get down to it —what's the secret of baseball?" He thought for a moment, then replied, "Consistency is the mark of greatness." Tighe was sitting at the other end of the bench. Without looking up, he said, "What if you're consistently horseshit?"

I remember Tighe's first talk to these young players. The camp was located next to an airfield and Tighe, sounding very serious, said, "Men, you are here to do well and we want you to do well. But I give you one word of caution. If any player asks you to chase a ball out on the runway, don't do it. It means he wants your job."

Bill Norman, another minor league manager, succeeded Tighe, and if Tighe was in over his head, this poor man was inundated. He was completely out of his element. He had little grasp of the major league scene, and the only interesting thing he ever said was, "Some days you win, some days you lose, and some days it rains." It was a terrific quote—the first time. The 303rd time, it wasn't so good. He said it every day.

Norman was fired after one month of the 1959 season. The Tigers had gotten off to a horrible start, going 2-15, and this was when I knew that Edgar Hayes, my boss at *The Detroit Times,* was a terrific reporter.

The Tigers were playing a Saturday game against the lowly Washington Senators, and the Senators were beating them badly. I was sitting on one side of the press box and Hayes on the other. He walked over to me in about the sixth inning and said, "They're going to fire the manager."

I looked at him.

"How do you know that?"

Edgar said, "It's going to happen. You stay here and I'll go back to the office and get the pages ready for the story."

He left, leaving me mystified. But I did not say anything. That's because I didn't know anything.

After the game—another bad loss—the Tigers called a hasty press conference and said Norman was being relieved of his duties as manager and Jimmy Dykes, who was coaching at Pittsburgh, would take over the next day, a doubleheader at home against the Yankees.

This happened on my birthday, May 2. Everyone at home was waiting for me so we could have a party. I knew I couldn't make it. We worked on the story until 11 o'clock. Jerry Green and I went back to the ball park at eight o'clock to see if anything was new. We thought some players might be still hanging around, and they were. Several, including Al Kaline, were still there. Norman was still in his office. He was roaring drunk, talking to no one and everyone.

Jerry and I looked in at him.

Kaline said, "Why don't you leave him alone?"

He was right, of course. I felt like a vulture. It was a feeling I still haven't forgotten.

When I got back to the office for the second time, I asked Edgar how he knew they were going to fire Norman.

He said, "I know where all the officials like to sit, in which part of the ball park. When I saw their seats were empty, I knew something was up. I figured they'd all gone back to the front office and were going to do something about the manager."

Which is the sort of newspapering that doesn't happen too often.

The next day, the Yankees came in for the doubleheader and Norman watched from the press box. The Tigers beat the Yankees twice as Charley Maxwell hit four home runs. I didn't go near Norman. I didn't know what to ask him and I didn't want to bring him anymore grief after what I had done the day before.

Dykes was fun, certainly refreshing. He had an impish sense of humor and because he had been around so long, he knew the situation in Detroit was almost impossible, so he handled it all in a light-handed way. His stories from the past were wonderful.

In a very short time, the whole thing got to Dykes, until a year later he suffered the indignity of being sent to Cleveland for Joe Gordon in the only trade of managers in history. Dykes liked to smoke cigars. He was smoking them all the time. The day of the trade we sat in his room and asked him how he felt. He said he felt fine, just fine, what's the problem? But I noticed one thing. He kept drumming his fingers on the back of the sofa. He never showed any emotion. I noticed another thing. He forgot to light his cigar.

Gordon was a good guy, a fun guy. I liked having him around because I grew up in New York when he was the second baseman of the Yankees, and I could ask him about the great players on that team: DiMaggio, Keller, Henrich, Rizzuto and Rolfe. But, quicker than all the others, he saw no hope, no future, in Detroit, and quit at the end of the season. He didn't last two months.

Bob Scheffing, the old Cubs' catcher, took over in 1961 (after I had hired Bill Rigney the previous October) and he was a beautiful man. Friendly. Classy. Caring. With the right kind of stories and the right approach to his game. For the first time, I felt the Tigers had the perfect manager.

They contended in 1961, pushing the Yankees all the way into September, until they lost a three-game series in New York and, in

10 days, fell from a half game out to 10½ games out. It was still a terrific season, with one upsetting moment.

I was on the outs with Rocky Colavito and when we got to Los Angeles for a series against the Angels in May, I got into a conversation with Rigney, who was now managing the Angels. The Tigers were beating everyone in sight and Rigney kept needling me how they would have it all wrapped up by Mother's Day.

Not quite, I told him.

Why not, he said.

I told him: "Steve Boros is going great at third, but there is no guarantee he can keep it up. The same with Norm Cash at first (who went on to the batting title.)" I listed what I thought were the potential trouble spots on the team, and Sam Greene, the old writer, was standing there chomping on the stub end of a cigar and added, "And there is always Colavito," meaning he couldn't be counted on either. I told Rigney what I thought were the positive things about the club and we all had a laugh over the whole thing and forgot about it until the next day.

I did not know that standing nearby was John Hall, a Los Angeles columnist. He eavesdropped on the entire conversation and chose to write only the negative things I had said—nothing positive. The Colavito line stood out above all others. Hall neglected to mention this was Sam's contribution, not mine, and so you can imagine the reaction when the players read his column, which was headlined: "Writer Blasts Tigers."

Colavito had to be furious, though he never said a word to me. I went to Scheffing to explain what had happened—how Hall had listened in and only quoted the unfavorable things I had said. Scheffing asked what I wanted him to do.

"I want you to call a clubhouse meeting and explain exactly what happened, or else I'm going to get killed," I told him.

He said, "Consider it done."

I felt a little better, but not much better. Later on, I felt awful. I learned Scheffing never said a word to his players. I still liked him and felt bad that he did not have it in him to talk to them. Two years later, he was fired, but he really quit on himself, and Jim Campbell, the general manager, had no choice but to let him go.

Campbell brought in Charlie Dressen, the old warhorse, figuring what his team needed was some veteran leadership. He was colorful, all right. In spring training he had his coaches chopping onions and peeling potatoes after practice. Dressen considered himself a chef, and not an amateur chef, either. He would bring forth his

specialities to the press room after practice. His favorite was chili—
"Charlie's Chili"—and it was very good. He would chortle as we each
paid him our compliments.

One day he thought he would try his famous cherry cobbler. We
thought we would try something of our own. We would tell him,
thank you, but no thank you—we don't care for any. When he walked
in with a big pan of his latest creation, we all begged off, saying we
were full or saving ourselves for dinner.

Dressen didn't catch on until the fifth or sixth refusal. He figured it out. "Damn you guys" he said, and threw the cobbler against
the bar and walked out of the room. The laughter went on all night.

The tough stuff was to follow. In his third season on the job
Dressen got up early one morning in Lakeland and called the room
of Stubby Overmire, one of his coaches.

"I need a favor," Dressen said.

"What's that?" asked Overmire, still waking up.

"I want you to drive me to the airport."

"The airport?"

"Yes. How soon can you get dressed?"

Dressen had suffered a heart attack during the night. He did
not want to tell anyone, least of all Jim Campbell, his boss. He wanted
to get on a plane and fly back to Los Angeles where he could see his
own doctor. That's exactly what he did, and was lost to the team for
the rest of the season.

He came back in 1966 and suffered another heart attack, and
he eventually died. Coach Bob Swift took his place, as he had done
the previous year, but he, too, fell victim to an illness and died of
cancer at the end of the season. Frank Skaff, a longtime and faithful
scout of the Tigers, finished out the season as the third manager of
the year.

Campbell picked Mayo Smith as his next manager. No one in
Detroit knew much about him, except he had managed the Phillies
in 1955-57. Campbell liked the older managers.

Smith was a perfect fit in Detroit. He didn't do much managing.
The Tigers had some talented players by now and he let them play.
They missed the pennant on the final day of the 1967 season, then
won it all in 1968. That's when Smith made the move of a lifetime,
putting centerfielder Mickey Stanley at shortstop in the World Series
so that the injured Al Kaline could reclaim his place in rightfield.

Smith was known as "America's Guest." He could eat and drink
with the best of them. He just never bought. He could be seen in
press rooms all over the league, enjoying himself late into the night.

On the day he was fired after the 1970 season, he went at it pretty good and wound up saying: "The fans in Detroit know as much about baseball as Chinese aviators." It was his most colorful comment.

It was here that Campbell made the biggest compromise of his life. He brought in Billy Martin. He knew he would be trouble, but figured Martin knew how to handle a club for a couple years before his problems got out of hand. The Tigers won the Eastern Division in 1972, before losing to Oakland in the playoffs. Campbell's move paid off. But not for long. He fired Martin the next year when Martin's behavior was too much to tolerate. Martin was a devious man, not very likeable, and when he died, I wrote this. I got a ton of mail castigating me for saying unkind things after a man was dead. I didn't get it. How could dying make him a better man? It was an argument I couldn't win, and didn't.

The old guard—Al Kaline, Norm Cash, Willie Horton, Dick McAuliffe, Bill Freehan and Gates Brown—were fading away, and Campbell knew it. He brought in his friend, Ralph Houk, the former Yankee manager, thinking he could keep things quiet when the Tigers dropped in the standings. They dropped all the way to last in 1975, losing 19 in a row at one point and winding up with 102 losses. Houk could do nothing about it but was a calm influence...except for that night in Toronto.

Houk was having his problems with Willie Horton. Willie was in a sulk. Houk wanted him to pinch hit against the Blue Jays but Horton couldn't be found. He was back in the clubhouse.

You must understand this: Ralph Houk has the most violent temper of any man I have ever known. He can be peaceful and placid for long periods of time, but when he blew up, it was like a volcano. This I didn't know.

He was still bristling about Horton when Campbell took us to dinner that night—me, Houk and Rick Ferrell. They talked about Willie and I stayed out of the conversation. Finally, Houk asked me: "What would you do with Willie Horton?"

I told him I'd put him in the lineup, play him every day and bat him cleanup.

Houk lunged for me across the table. Ferrell was able to knock his arm away. Houk started screaming and everyone in the restaurant looked at us. Campbell said, "We'd better get out of here."

We walked back to the hotel in pairs: Campbell and Houk ahead, Ferrell and I well behind. Houk kept turning around and glaring at me. Campbell had to restrain him several times.

It was a very scary moment.

The next day, I saw Houk in the dugout and he said, "Hi, Joe. How are you doing today?"

I told him fine. I was still shaking from the previous day.

Campbell was a good man—my favorite of all the people I ever wrote about. We battled. I called him stubborn, he called me narrow. But it never got out of hand. He had more integrity than any man I ever knew.

After Houk, Campbell felt he should promote Les Moss from the minors and make him the manager in 1979. It was a thoughtful gesture but lasted little more than a month. Moss was a wonderful person but was in the wrong job. You knew he was going to have his problems when, on the opening day of spring training at the minor league base in Tigertown, he let the fans on the field. His players couldn't even play catch for fear of hitting one of them with a ball.

Campbell was in Los Angeles for a game when he saw Sparky Anderson sitting in the press room. Anderson had been let out by the Cincinnati Reds and Campbell knew what he had to do: he hired Sparky and let Moss go. It was the right thing to do, but Campbell spoke for years about the unfair treatment he had given Moss. He never got over it.

Anderson lasted 17 seasons and was the finest man and manager I ever knew in the Detroit dressing room. He had a grasp of everything, including people's feelings, and got along with everyone. Now it is Buddy Bell's turn and I wrote a paragraph about him in his first training camp that truly surprised myself. I wrote, "I find I am liking this man quicker than all the other managers we've had in Detroit."

High praise. But this is a very special man—a man without motive or ego. A friendly man, a dedicated man—a man with a sense of humor, which he will need in the years to come.

My wife, Mary Jane, pets her favorite guy, Secretariat, at Claiborne Farm in Paris, Kentucky. She used to like me better but found out Big Red ran faster and made more money.

Here I am with my No. 1 man, all time, in 50 years of writing sports: Jim Campbell, General Manager and president of the Detroit Tigers. No wonder we got along—look at those hats.

My son, Mike Falls, age 7, and his favorite ball player, Vida Blue of the Oakland A's. Mike's favorite team was the Houston Astros. Huh?

Ralph Houk, Tiger manager in the 1970s, and I talk in one of his quieter moments. This was before he tried to punch me out in a Toronto restaurant.

The Detroit News took this picture of me and my wife as we walked down the steps of Michigan Stadium. It was titled: "Joe Falls and his Fan Club."

My favorite sports writers at a gas station gathering in Traverse City, Michigan. Left to right: Mike Sturm, *Bay City Times;* Al Cotton, *Jackson Citizen-Patriot;* George Alderton, *Lansing State Journal,* me, and Doug Mintline, *Flint Journal.* All are gone. Alderton, 90 in this picture, was the man who gave the Michigan State Spartans their nickname.

Me and my staff members at the press table of the NBA All-Star game at the Silverdome in Pontiac. That's Bill Halls and Jerry Green to my left. I'm wearing dark glasses because the fans kept confusing me with Larry Bird and asking for my autograph.

Me, the sailor, at the end of his second Port Huron to Mackinac sailboat race on Mackinac Island. My hair turned white when I fell overboard and my shipmates told me not to worry: "Go stand under a shade tree!"

This is the end of the Boston Marathon and Jerry Coyle (left) and Bob Keiss are finishing in a tie for 9,347th place. I dedicated my book on the Boston Marathon to them, calling them "two fast friends."

If I seem like a happy man in this picture, it is because I had always had a lifelong dream to visit Carnoustie in Northern Scotland—the scene of Ben Hogan's only appearance in the British Open. Ben, of course, won the tournament for his third straight major in 1953 but instead of going for golf's Grand Slam, he went home to sit on his porch in Texas because he was tired of golf.

Here I am, the Pulitzer Prize-winning golf writer, striking my best pose in the press tent of the British Open at St. Andrews. This man has it all: a Scottish hat, dark glasses, a press tag, a copy of the *Paris Tribune* and an old-fashioned typewriter. Everything but the Pulitzer Prize.

This is one of my greatest bosses, Ed Hayes, former sports editor of the *Detroit Times*. Ed, retired and in a wheelchair, taught me as much about journalism—how to find good stories—as anyone in my 50 years of writing sports.

A good day in Detroit: Sam Bishop, the longtime coach at Northwestern High School in Detroit, is honored at a United Foundations luncheon after he had retired. Bishop did his job for 45 years, working with young men, black and white, showing them the way in life. Bishop wound up in the Michigan Sports Hall of Fame.

Here I am with my auto insurance man. His name is Johnny Mowers and I was having a party for him in Dearborn. Mowers also played goal for the Detroit Red Wings and won the Vezina Trophy as the league's best goalie in 1942.

A good moment: a chance to interview Maurice Richard, former firebrand of the Montreal Canadiens, at an "Original Six" hockey tournament in Toronto. The Rocket's eyes would light up like two hot coals when he barged in on the net and they did the same on this day. That's when I asked him why he was afraid of Gordie Howe. (Only kidding, Rocket. Only kidding.)

Here I am with my oldest son, No. 95, Rob Falls, of the North Farmington football team. No. 95 didn't play much; just one play in three years on the varsity. He had two major knee oprations and was on crutches nine different times. It was all worth it. When he went away to school at Eastern Michigan, he vowed he would never touch drugs and never did, crediting not me or his mother or his parish priest or his counselor, but football coach Ron Holland, the man who never played him.

Mary Jane at Wimbledon—prettier, even, than the flowers.

Sherlock Holmes, on the right, is displaying some rare affection for his roommate. No, that's not Dr. Watson.

My longtime mentor, Sam Greene, baseball writer of *The Detroit News.* When I was 30, Sam was 60, and Sam taught me how to behave myself in my job by simply being nice to people, which Sam did in his every waking hour. He could also outwrite me.

Me and Tommy McCarthy, the longtime press box attendant at Fenway Park in Boston. This was Tommy's 53rd anniversary on the job, so I went to a Boston bank and got him 53 new one dollar bills. I told him: "I just hope you don't make it to 100."

A gourmet of great renown, here I am trying to get into Maxim's in Paris. They heard I was coming and locked the door.

One of the my best friends, Doug Mintline, sports editor of the *Flint Journal*, at the Buick Open in Grand Blanc, Michigan. Doug gave me the greatest advice I ever received as a newsman: "Nothing takes the place of good stories."

The spring training gang at Henley Field in Lakeland (circa 1960): (L to R)—Bob Reynolds, WJR; Hal Middlesworth, Tigers' PR; Van Patrick, broadcaster; me; Doug Mintline, *Flint Journal;* Ray Lane, radio-TV; Jim Hendrick, radio; Watson Spoelstra, *Detroit News;* and Jack Slayton, *Lakeland Ledger.*

Braves Field in Boston, former home of the Boston Braves (one time known as the Boston Bees). The place is gone. All that's left is the ticket office across the street.

Here I am telling Don Canham, athletic director at the University of Michigan, that his hot dogs in the press box are soggy. Canham told me: "Pack a lunch."

Rocky Marciano, reigning heavyweight champion, shakes my hand while training in Holland, Michigan, for a fight with Jersey Joe Walcott in the early 1950s. Marciano looks a little amused, saying, "You look like a high school student instead of a sportswriter."

Don't Knock The Rock. Not anymore. After years of squabbling with each other, Rocky Colavito and I are old buddies in a meeting in Colavito's hotel room at the Book Cadillac in Detroit. Colavito is smiling because I haven't asked him yet why he popped up so much with the bases loaded.

Here I am in my first training camp with the Tigers in Lakeland. It is 1956 and I am writing home to my wife and children and telling them how much I miss them.

This is the lighthouse at Turnberry, Scotland, one of the venues for the British Open. We are showing it because you're probably tired of seeing pictures of Joe.

Time to say goodbye. Gordie Howe, the great star of the Detroit Red Wings, and I show up for one last look at old Olympia Stadium on Grand River in Detroit before they tear it down. I am wearing the hard hat. Howe didn't need one—not after all those pucks bounced off his head.

Mary Jane and I posing for a picture at the Palace of Versailles outside of Paris. I thought it was a nice place, but they didn't have enough lights hanging from the ceilings.

And now we give you the star of our family—young Leslie, my daughter, on a train in Great Britain. If you wonder why she seems so happy, I was late and missed the train, and Leslie and her mom had a nice weekend in Edinborough.

Chapter 10:
Boo on Bo

The two most interesting football coaches were Woody Hayes of Ohio State and Bo Schembechler of Michigan. When I would cover one of their games, I would not follow the cheerleaders through my binoculars. I kept the glasses on the coaches. You never knew what they were going to do—when the next eruption was going to take place. They never let you down.

I knew Woody first. The Skywriters' tour of the Big Ten football camps always made Columbus the last stop. Woody was always a show. We would interview all the other coaches but not this man. He would take us into one of the classrooms and lecture us, usually on some military battle of the past. Once in a while, he'd talk football. He tolerated no questions.

One year we went to Columbus and the gates to the practice field were closed. We went for help but nobody could get them open. Woody was not about to let us in. We'd been to 10 schools, including Notre Dame, and now we were being told we were not welcome. The guys were furious. You don't lock out 30 football writers. One, maybe. Two, maybe. But not 30. Everyone was fuming on the bus ride back to the airport. I didn't care because I knew what Hayes was doing. He was upstaging the other 10 coaches. He knew this would make a sweet story. Besides, he knew some of our readers would enjoy the fact we were rebuffed.

The next year, Ohio State was last on the schedule again. This time we were ready. We phoned ahead and had a hardware store bring a big ladder to the practice field. It wasn't needed.

The gates were wide open and Hayes was standing there smiling!

"Welcome, gentlemen. Where have you been? Welcome to Ohio State University. If we can be of any service to you, please let us know. We are here to please you."

He had his team in full dress uniform and each player stepped forward and saluted us while giving his name, position and home town. Hayes had beach chairs and umbrella tables set up. He had cookies and cold drinks on the tables. Woody had done it again—he'd upstaged every coach in the conference, including Notre Dame.

Hayes knew who I was but never called me by name. I came from that terrible state to the north. One year I drove to Columbus for his Monday press conference before the Michigan-Ohio State game. This was an important moment for the Ohio media—the only real chance they had to talk to the Buckeyes' coach all week long. He would give them 10 minutes after Thursday night's practice but this was when they would get their pictures, tapes and comments.

The room was packed with the press. TV cameras were arrayed in a semicircle, aimed at the rostrum. Tape recorders were in place. Hayes came out and the room grew silent. The cameras were rolling.

Hayes looked around and said, "I am sorry but there will be no press conference today since a member of the enemy is in the audience."

And he walked out.

Everyone was flustered. No press conference? No comments? What would they do for their TV and radio shows, much less the newspapers? We all looked around, wondering what was going on.

Who was this member of the enemy?

The enemy was me. If you've ever had a roomful of writers, reporters and broadcasters glare at you because you've robbed them of their stories, you haven't missed a thing.

Another time I was in Ann Arbor on the Friday before the big game. I decided I'd go out to the stadium to see what was going on. Bad move.

It was about four o'clock in the afternoon and Ohio State was going through its final walk-through. I was the only one in the stadium —me and 100,000 empty seats.

Hayes saw me and came storming over.

"What are you doing here?" he bellowed.

Oh, my.

"I always go to practice," I said.

"You do? Why do you go to practice?" He was furious.

"So I can learn things."

"And what do you learn?"

"I learn not to go to practice."

He didn't laugh. I left.

You could not get mad at this man. He was a blunderbuss. A determined, dedicated blunderbuss. I wound up on his bus going to a game at Iowa City. Don't ask me how it happened but I was in the seat behind him. Forest Evashevski, a bit of a scallywag himself, was the Iowa coach and he was more than ready for the invasion of Woody and his Buckeyes. He let the grass grow from the 20-yard lines in at both ends of the field, hoping to slow down the Ohio State runners. Remember: It was four yards and a cloud of dust. Hayes went off the pad when he saw the field conditions. He ordered his assistants to go out and bring back some lawn mowers. Not many places sold lawn mowers in November, so Hayes did the next best thing. It was a freezing day and he went over to the Iowa bench during the game and stole one of their heaters.

Years later, after Hayes had been fired for striking a Clemson player at a bowl game, my office asked me to do a piece on him. What could be new? I called the Ohio State publicity department and spoke to Marv Homan, the man in charge.

"I need a Woody story."

"I've got one," he whispered over the phone. Homan knew his place. You were very careful about the way you talked about Wayne Woodrow Hayes. Hayes had been given an office in the ROTC building next to St. John's Arena and Homan told of the time Hayes drove his truck to work.

"I could hear a racket going on outside the window, so I peeked through the curtain," he said. "There was Woody trying to get his truck into the last parking space. He was furious. He'd pull in carefully but when he tried to open the door, it hit against the car next to him and he couldn't get out. He backed up and tried again but again the door wouldn't open. Finally, he backed out one more time and got out of the truck and pushed it into the vacant spot."

Schembechler worked for Hayes at Ohio State, first as a graduate assistant, then as an assistant coach, and finally as his offensive coordinator. They fought all the time. They were arguing about something or another and Schembechler threw a chair at Hayes. He missed. They would play racquetball on Sunday mornings and Hayes wouldn't quit until he got the best of his young coach, which seldom happened.

Schembechler said, "We'd play two out of three, then he'd make it three out of five, then four out of seven and five out of nine. He'd stay there all day and night until he was on top."

Bo laughed, "I never let him get on top."

Bo liked Woody, and when Hayes was fired by Ohio State, Bo went right to his side. He drove through a heavy snowstorm and met Hayes in Bowling Green, about halfway between Ann Arbor and Columbus, at the home of Doyt Perry, an old coach who was friends with both men.

Schembechler did not chastise Hayes for his actions but told him that he had to apologize. He told him: "That's a must. You've got to say you're sorry."

Hayes promised to do so, but never did. That hurt Schembechler, but he said no more about it.

Ohio State hammered Michigan 50-20 in 1961. Schembechler was calling the plays from the press box. He got all kinds of criticism for rolling up the score. Not right. The phones to the bench went out in the third quarter and it was Hayes who called the plays.

"That was Woody, all right," Schembechler said. "We had the game blown out, so he was going to take over and make a big show of it. He marched up and down the sidelines so everyone could see him."

I once wrote a book with Schembechler. It was after he had suffered a heart attack at the 1970 Rose Bowl. I thought it would make good reading, detailing how a man overcomes such a thing and goes on to be a success.

Bo spoke into a tape recorder and we were doing fine until the day he said, "That's it. I'm done. I'm not going to talk about myself anymore."

And he didn't.

The book was only half finished and I didn't know what to do. So I did the only thing left: I talked to everybody else—his wife, his coaches, his players, his trainers, his doctors, his equipment man...even Woody. He told me Bo was a good boy and one day might make a football coach.

When these two would play each other, they'd meet at midfield for a friendly chat. But neither would cross the 50 and go into the other's territory. They always kept their distance.

Not many knew it, but Schembechler married Woody's secretary. The marriage didn't last long. As we were working on the book, I told Bo we would have to mention the marriage and he said, "No way, that's not going in there!"

I turned off the recorder. "Bo, if we don't mention this—and it'll just be a bare mention—people will wonder what else we've left out, and the book will lose its credibility."

He saw my logic and said, "Ok, let's go."

I turned the recorder back on. "What was your first wife's name?"

Bo looked across the desk at me.

"Bo, the name of your first wife!"

He was silent

"Come on..."

He rose from his chair and pointed his finger at me and said, "Dammit...I remember she liked horses."

Schembechler's first season at Michigan was a wild one. He came in almost a complete unknown. Van Patrick, the TV man, broke the story. When he said, "The next coach of the Michigan football team will be Bo Schembechler," very few of us knew who he was talking about.

What was that second name again? How do you spell it? How do you pronounce it?

Schembechler had been coach at Miami of Ohio, and virtually everyone forgot he once worked for Woody at Ohio State. There was only one coaching story in Columbus, and it did not involve any of the assistants.

Bo worked hard that first season in Ann Arbor, too hard. He was trying to coach and recruit at the same time. He was up against the popular Duffy Daugherty at Michigan State and if there was one thing Duffy could do it was lure top prospects to East Lansing.

Schembechler would be out until two o'clock in the morning on the recruiting trail, often stopping for a couple of hamburgers before going home. This was after his 12-hour days coaching the team. He was getting heavier and heavier.

On the Tuesday before the Ohio State game, the Michigan campus was hit by an ice storm and the practice field was frozen over. Schembechler could not have been more dismayed. Tuesday, Wednesday and Thursday were the days coaches got the job done; now he faced the prospect of losing all three days. The Wolverines did not have their indoor practice facility yet.

So there was Bo, along with the groundskeepers, his assistant coaches, and the assistant athletic director, chopping away at the ice all through the day. They were able to clear enough away to get in their three sessions. On Friday night, Schembechler took his team into a downtown hotel in Ann Arbor so the players would get their proper rest.

In the middle of the night, the furnaces went out. Bo was up and screaming for the hotel to get the heat back on. He started passing out blankets to his players before he ran out of them. He finally said, "The hell with it" and went to bed. That afternoon, Michigan upset Ohio State, the No. 1 team in the nation, 24-12, and a great coaching career was underway...with a few detours.

When we went to the Rose Bowl, I thought Bo was acting pretty strange. He seemed very nervous, almost jittery. One day he took a football and raced all over the field, as if to show everyone everything was all right with him.

But everything wasn't all right.

He was still heavy, and he looked drained. One night, in a press conference at the Sheraton Huntington Hotel in Pasadena, I asked about his health.

He glared at me.

"I'm OK, you hear? I'm just fine. There is nothing wrong with me! You got me?"

I wrote something was wrong with the Michigan football coach and I feared for his health. Two days later he had his heart attack.

It happened when Bo took his team to a monastery on the side of a mountain. He wanted to give his players some privacy.

I was working for *The Detroit Free Press* and we got to the press box early—three or four hours before the game. That's how you do it at big events. Don't get caught in the traffic.

With about two hours to go, they made an announcement over the P.A. system: "Attention, press. Bo Schembechler has the flu and will not be accompanying Michigan to the Rose Bowl today."

I looked at Curt Sylvester, our college football writer, and said, "That's a lot of baloney. They'd have to cut his legs off at the knees to keep him away from this game. Something is wrong."

But what?

We looked around the press box, especially where the Michigan officials would sit. Their seats were empty. This added to the mystery but didn't help us find out anything.

Curt said he talked to a young reporter from the *Michigan Daily* and she said Tom Maentz, one of the Michigan players, told her that Schembechler had suffered a heart attack and was in the hospital. A big story but not enough information to write it.

When the assistant coaches came up and went into their booth, I could see George Mans crying. Dramatic but still not enough to write a story. The Michigan doctors were on the field but, knowing doctors, I knew they wouldn't say anything. The Michigan officials were not back in their seats, so we had to wait until the end of the game to find out what was going on.

Michigan lost, 10-3, and a horde of writers and broadcasters went into the press room to talk to the Michigan doctors.

They hemmed and hawed, talking all around the subject, until Pete Waldmeir, columnist for *The Detroit News,* blurted out: "Did Bo Schembechler have a heart attack?"

When they said yes, there was a stampede out of the press room. With a three-hour time difference, we didn't have much time to do our stories. Curt and I must have written for two hours straight. We felt exhausted, but satisfied, at the end of the day.

Schembechler had a glorious career at Michigan. He didn't have much success in the bowl games but he took Michigan back to the old heights—a worthy successor to Fielding H. Yost and Fritz Crisler. He was a winner.

We got along well. He told me one day: "You know less about football than any writer I've ever known, but you are the most honest newspaperman I've ever known."

This was one of the great compliments of my life.

I did get mad at this man more than once, but I'm not sure it meant anything to him.

When he was nearing his 20th year at Michigan, I went out to see him at practice, and after we'd had dinner at the training table, I told him: "It's time for us to do another book. You've done an awful lot and we ought to bring it all up to date or write a new one."

"I will not do any more books until I am done coaching," he said. "I don't want that in my life."

I told him, OK, but when the time came, I would like to do it.

The next year, we were back at the Rose Bowl and I was sitting in the press room working on my column. Some guy came around with a press release. It said that Bo Schembechler, coach of the Michigan football team, was writing a book with Mitch Albom, columnist of *The Detroit Free Press,* and it would be out late next summer.

I froze.

I could feel the heat working up in my face but didn't dare say anything. I would not say anything at all, not until after the game. I did not want to be charged with upsetting this man.

On the plane ride home, I asked Schembechler if I could talk to him in the galley. I said, "I thought you told me you were not going to write anymore books until you were finished coaching."

"He offered me $160,000," he said. "I'm going to put it all in to our new football building."

I said, "You don't think I couldn't get you $160,000?" Bo just looked at me, and I turned away and left. I hated to think about it, but they say every man has his price. His was $160,000.

When Schembechler suffered another heart attack and nearly died, the Michigan people asked the media if we would not bother Bo in his recovery. The school said he would talk to everyone at the same time when the time was right.

That made sense, but I also knew what could happen. So, I spoke to Don Canham, the athletic director, Bruce Madej, the sports information director, and even Bo's wife, Millie. I told them my newspaper would go along with this request, but we did not want someone walking up to Bo's house, ringing the doorbell, and getting an exclusive interview.

They all promised this would not happen.

When Michigan played in The Gator Bowl, there was Bo jabbering away on TV about the game, his team and his health problems. He had broken his word to us. When I asked him about it, he said, "Hey, that was TV. That was big."

The third strike came after he left Michigan and became president of the Detroit Tigers.

Bo had more than his share of detractors. Some thought he was a bully. A dictator. A nasty guy. I liked him because I thought he was an honest, hard-working guy who would never cheat. When he took the Tigers' job, he was not a very big favorite, especially among the Michigan State backers. They would like to see him fail in baseball because they could never get the best of him in football.

Ernie Harwell was the Tigers' broadcaster. He'd been on the job for more than 30 years and was probably the most popular sports figure in Michigan. Everyone liked Ernie, who was a very likable man.

When it was announced he was being let go after one more year in the radio booth, the press and public went into an uproar. A lot of people couldn't believe the Tigers would do this to Harwell.

Ernie called a press conference before Christmas and cried to the media, saying there was nothing wrong with him, not with his eyes, his voice or anything else. He did not appreciate the treatment he was getting from the Tigers. He called the press conference in the Tigers' own press room, then drilled the team that had employed him for so long.

It was a spectacular story. Everyone shot Schembechler between the eyes, thinking this was his decision. People called into radio stations and wrote letters to the newspapers. It was the biggest public reaction anyone had ever seen in Detroit.

Even Albom, who had co-authored a book with Bo, came down on Schembechler with a scathing column.

I'd have probably done the same thing except I was home with the flu. I had several days to think before giving my reaction. Something didn't feel right about the story.

Then it hit me. All we were getting was Harwell's side. It made great news—very personal, very emotional. How could they do this to our Ernie?

I thought, "Why aren't the Tigers talking?"

It dawned on me that Harwell had agreed to a final year in a meeting the previous October. He had accepted the Tigers' offer. If he didn't like what they were doing, that was the time to say so, not in a one-man press conference in the Christmas season. I figured he had three choices: 1. He could accept their offer. 2. He could tell them he wanted better. 3. Or he could leave.

He took their offer and so it didn't seem right, or fair, to cry about it later in public.

This is what I wrote for Sunday, and it made absolutely no impression on the public. Everyone loved Ernie and the facts meant nothing to them.

The Tigers—especially Schembechler—took a terrific beating in the ensuing weeks. They were made to look like the all-time Scrooges. Jim Campbell was furious with Ernie. He figured him as an employee and did not appreciate him making the Tigers look so bad. Everyone got it in the front office, even the secretaries.

The whole thing was completely out of hand.

The story still bothered me. I did not feel we knew everything. So I kept digging. I found out that it was Schembechler who fought for Harwell, getting him one more year at the mike, at more money than Ernie had ever earned. He wouldn't come forth on his behalf and say these things because he was still being Bo Schembechler, the hard head.

I found out it was Jim Long, a nice man who ran radio station WJR, who wanted Harwell out. I found this hard to believe because Long had always been such a quiet man, a gentle man. I did not see how he could make such a bold decision. If it were not for Bo, Harwell would have been gone on the spot. What Long didn't like about Ernie, I could not find out. But his dislike was very clear, and very strong.

I went to Schembechler's office and said, "Bo, this whole thing is getting ridiculous. You're getting blamed for everything and that's not right."

He said, "I'm the boss and I'll take the heat."

"Fine," I said. "But you're getting killed, and more than that, this story has been twisted out of shape. The public should know what's going on."

Once again, he saw my logic. He said, "OK, I'll make a deal with you. I'll tell you everything that happened, in detail, and you can use it if you don't quote me. And I won't talk to anyone else about it. I'll tell them it's all in your story."

I told him: "I'll use it if I can get it confirmed by another source."

We agreed to meet in the basement of Campbell's house the next night. Campbell would stay out of it.

We spent a couple of hours going over everything. I didn't tell Bo where I would get it confirmed. It would be Long. Bo had said, "He's the guy who did it, and he's a no good so-and-so if he won't own up to it."

The next day, a Friday, I told my office I might have a story on the Harwell firing, which was a mistake on my part. I felt I knew Jim Long well enough that when I confronted him with what I knew, he would tell me the truth. My office got very excited about the prospect of a page one story, especially since this was the only news which seemed to exist in our city.

I called Long about three o'clock in the afternoon and told him what I knew. I didn't tell him where I got the information.

He listened, then said, "Joe, you know me. How many years have we known each other? Do you think I would do something like that to a man like Ernie Harwell?"

I hung up the phone feeling defeated. My office called. How was the story coming? All the execs were anxiously waiting for it.

I told them give me a little more time. I didn't think that would help. I thought the story was dead. But I had to tell them something.

So I sat in my office at home, feeling lower and lower by the moment, when the phone rang. It was about seven o'clock. My bosses were still waiting to hear from me.

I picked up the phone.

"Hello."

"Hello, Joe. Jim Long. I had to call you. After we spoke this afternoon, I took the long way home. I live in Grosse Pointe but I went all over the place thinking of our conversation. I can't keep it in any longer. I fired Ernie Harwell. Not Bo, me. I did it."

Then he told me the story.

We bannered it across the top of our Sunday paper and it made terrific reading. We beat everyone on the story. They all started scrambling to catch up. Bob Talbert, a columnist for *The Free Press,* seemed especially upset. He went on TV and said, "Why isn't Joe Falls on television confirming his story?" Why did I have to confirm anything to TV? Bob probably felt it couldn't be right until it was on television. Shows you how our business has changed.

Obviously, I felt pretty good...until I picked up *The Detroit Free Press* the next day. Here was a big story by Mitch Albom on the whole situation—all from Bo Schembechler. He quoted Bo from top to bottom. I couldn't believe my eyes. What happened to our deal? We agreed he would tell me everything but I couldn't quote him and he would talk to no else. Now he was being quoted all over the place.

I called Bo at his home.

He said, "Well, one of my sons saw him walking up to the house and said, 'Mitch Albom is here.' I told him not to let him in."

And..."

"He came in anyway and we talked."

"You said you wouldn't talk to anyone."

"I didn't know I was being quoted."

"Did he have a tape recorder with him."

"Yes."

"Was it turned on."

"I guess so."

"You guess so?"

"I didn't know what he was up to. I didn't know he was recording anything."

I don't remember the rest of the conversation. I didn't feel bad for myself, just for Bo. He had broken his word for the third time, and I never thought he'd even do it once.

But, we all survive and go on and I'm not mad at him. I figure he is just Bo and can't help himself playing the part. Besides, most folks still blame him for dumping Harwell.

Chapter 11:
26 Miles, 385 Yards

I like to read out of town papers to see what other guys are writing, and how they do it. What better way to learn? My favorite sports writers are Mike Downey of the *Los Angeles Times* (who works three times harder than anyone I know and has a great sense of humor), Dave Kindred, who writes out of Atlanta and does a column for *The Sporting News* (a man with a beautiful writing style I will never equal), Tom Boswell of the *Washington Post* (a great mind and clear thinker even if he roots too much for the Baltimore Orioles), and my two friends from the *Boston Globe,* both brilliant in their own way—Bob Ryan and Dan Shaughnessy. If I had two more sons, I'd pick these two, and of course, Jim Murray.

I was reading *NEWSDAY* one day and came across a column by Stan Isaacs, another favorite. I like writers who truly care about what they're doing instead of showing off. Stan wrote, "You cannot call yourself a compleat sports writer until you've covered the Boston Marathon."

The word "compleat" got to me. I always spelled it "complete," but I knew Stan was an educated guy and he probably had it right; I felt it was Olde English at work and I had great respect for it.

I wanted to be compleat, so I asked to cover the 1975 race and away I went to Boston. First, I did a column on some guy from Detroit who ran in the race. His name was Bob Keiss and he worked at one of our local colleges. He liked to run and listen to the radio. Get the weather. News. Pick up the Red Sox game in Fenway Park. I was fascinated.

When I got on the plane, Keiss and a friend of his, Dr. Jerry Coyle, a Detroit dentist, who was also a runner, were along with their wives. They said I would have to join them for dinner. They ate in the East End of Boston which was the Italian section. They said they had to load up on spaghetti, pack in those carbohydrates. Now I was even more fascinated. In my life, spaghetti was moving ahead of sex.

I was staying at the Sheraton Hotel, which was near the finish line, and when I went out to breakfast, I saw Catfish Hunter, the Yankee pitcher, crossing the street. He was the most celebrated baseball player of the time, having signed his big contract with the Yankees as a free agent and changing the face of the game. As he walked across the street, I noticed no one knew him—at least they were paying no attention to him. The kids were crowded around the competitors' busses, getting such treasured autographs as Richard Fritz, Fred Fletcher, Bruce Aldrich, Thomas Bleakley, John Walsh, Bill Zucker and Claude Fowler.

I took the press bus to Hopkinton for the start of the race. I had always seen those pictures of the runners snaking their way through the New England countryside, thousands and thousands of them. Now, here they were, all over the place, taking over the entire town of Hopkinton.

They were sitting on the lawns, walking along the sidewalks, some sitting up in trees in order to meditate. The lineups at the port-a-johns were immense. Some were peeing in the bushes. Men were putting grease on their nipples so they wouldn't get sore as their shirts rubbed against them during the race.

Never did I see a scene like this one. Soon, they all got into line and, at precisely noon, the gun went off to start the race. A guy called out: "Last one home is a rotten egg!"

Away they went, and I went along with them, riding in the back of the press bus. Not many guys covered the race, maybe a dozen. The pros sat there and waited until we neared the finish line before showing much interest in the race. I knelt on the back seat and looked out the back window, taken by the entire scene.

People were lined up all along the route, urging the runners along, applauding them, calling out their names, handing them cups of water.

The bus speeded up when we got near Boston. That's so we could get to the finish line at the Prudential Building. And here they came, one at a time, making it across the finish line while the fans cheered wildly.

The scene in the basement of the Prudential Building looked like something in the Crimean War. People were laying all over the floor. Some were leaning against walls, some were stretched out on chairs, some on tables. They were ashen in color. Some had their eyes closed. Some had glazed looks in their eyes. A lot were hurting. Doctors and nurses ministered to them and that's when I thought: "What the heck are they doing this for, anyway?" I had never seen so much pain in one place before.

The first runner I spoke to was a small woman, under five feet, who said her name was Sylvia Weiner and she came from Montreal.

"Why are you doing this?"

She looked up and managed a small smile. "I was in a concentration camp in Germany," she said, softly. "I saw my mother and father put to death. I survived. I always had a will to live but I never had any proof of my will. That's when I decided to run. I wanted to prove to myself that I could do something very difficult, so I taught myself to run."

The second runner I spoke to also was a woman. She said her named was Nina Kuscsick. She said she had just had a divorce and her husband got most of the property. He was a runner and she wanted to beat him, and did by 10 minutes or so.

Everyone had a similar story about why they were motivated to torture themselves in this manner. This was the only time in my life I had to force myself to leave the scene of an event because I was getting over-noted; I could never write all I was hearing.

It was coming clear to me. If you want to play in the World Series, too bad. You can't do it. The same for the Stanley Cup playoffs, Super Bowl or NBA playoffs. You had to be a special person to do those things.

But...if you wanted to run in the greatest footrace in the world and were willing to pay the price, you could do it.

This was a form of greatness, and it was available to everyone. Stan Isaacs had it exactly right.

The next day, I went to the library and asked if I could look at the books of the Boston Marathon. The woman at the desk went through her file system and said, "I'm sorry but there aren't any."

What? Not a book—not a word—on this great race?

Did I dare? Why not? Nobody else had done it, so I thought I should take a shot. I'd done two books, one on Bo Schembechler, the Michigan football coach, after his heart attack at the Rose Bowl and a history of the Detroit Tigers.

I knew that Jerry Nason of the *Boston Globe* was the recognized authority on the Boston Marathon. He had covered the race for years. He even put out a small pamphlet on the past winners. I knew I had to see him before I could go ahead. I felt it was his book, his area of expertise, and I could not do anything without his permission.

I called him up and he invited me to his house. What a gracious man. We had lunch and I told him of my plan, making it very clear that I felt he should be the one to write such a book.

He threw his hands into the air.

"Heavens, no. Not me," he said. "I'm too far along and couldn't take on such a project. But I'll be glad to help you any way I can."

He became my hero, my inspiration.

What we do as newspapermen is write daily stories. We report, we write, and then we do it all over the next day. Now, I took a whole week off and came back to Boston to get material for the book. I could not believe how much I could gather in seven days—so much that I put it in a trunk and then couldn't lift the trunk.

I spoke to everyone. Men. Women. Old runners. Young runners. Blind runners, even their dogs. All had a story to tell.

Joe Pardo was blind, but he ran in the race. When I went to see him, he took me out to a practice track. His seeing-eye dog was with him. He said, "You sit here in the bleachers and watch what happens at exactly three o'clock."

I sat down and Pardo started around the track. It was one o'clock in the afternoon. His dog sat at the side of the track, near the finish line.

Pardo went around and around. It got boring. I didn't dare say anything. I told myself I was seeing the essence of dedication.

It was getting close to three o'clock. Joe was still slogging along, almost walking but never breaking stride.

It was exactly three o'clock, and in that instant, his dog started barking. Time to quit. How could anyone believe such a thing?

I spoke to Johnny Kelly, who won the race in 1935 and 1945, and was still at it in his 70s. I spoke to Tommy Leonard, the bartender-runner, who always threw a big bash for the runners at the Eliot Lounge. What a good man. He loved the runners and he loved this race and he took me over the course, inch by inch, and filled me in on the history and tradition. I spoke to Red Auerbach, who was running the Boston Celtics and lived in the Lenox Hotel near the finish line. He thought they were all crazy. He said: "They go through all that for what, a plate of beef stew? They're nuts." I went to New York and spoke to Kathy Switzer, the second woman runner—the one who was pushed off the course by Jock Semple, one of the officials, who, in turn, was pushed off the course by one of the men runners.

When I got home, I thought I would play Ernest Hemingway. I got a cabin in the northern woods of Michigan, stocked it with food and drink, and sat down to write. I spread this material through all the rooms—on the tables, beds, chairs, the floor, refrigerator and stove. I wrote from sunrise to sunset, and then some. I finished the book in four days. My wife said, "Don't you dare tell anyone you did it that quickly."

I lucked out. I went to Macmillan publishers in New York, which had printed my Tiger history, and made a presentation. The editor was from Norway or Sweden—I forget which—and was taken by the idea. They had ski races in his country involving thousands of skiers and he figured if skiers were a good story, why not runners?

The book sold 40,000 copies and wound up on the *New York Times* bestseller list. I didn't put much stock in it because I knew the moment the next race was over, the book would fade from sight.

Not quite. Twenty years later I still hear from runners who enjoyed it. This is a little embarrassing because I can't remember all I wrote.

In any case, I wrote about running even before the great James Fixx came along with all of his books. I got in on it just as the sport was reaching its peak of interest. The book worked not because I wrote it so well but because I took the tack of saying: "What is it about these nutty people? What makes them run?" I let them all speak and that was the key. What did I know about this sport anyway? I can't run a temperature.

The runners liked me and I enjoyed this because I really didn't know much about running, least of all long-distance running. If I was bringing them some attention, fine. I knew they were getting very little of it.

When I came home, I wrote two pieces—one saying we should have a marathon in Detroit, the other saying we ought to bring the cars to Detroit and let them run through our streets. Both things came to pass but I never mentioned it again because it would come out as sounding self-serving. I simply suffered in silence.

My idea for a footrace was to make it an international event. I suggested they go over the Ambassador Bridge to Windsor and return through the Detroit-Windsor Tunnel. I guess I got this idea from the Grand Prix race at Monaco, where they race through the streets and go through that tunnel and come out by the Mediterranean Sea.

Anyway, my paper, *The Detroit Free Press*, decided to have a marathon in our city. I couldn't have been more pleased. My pleasure soon died when they went ahead with their plans and never talked to me. I was the only one who had any experience with marathons—I'd seen two or three by then—but they chose to do it on their own. I guess they wanted the credit.

Anyway, the marathon started in Windsor and came through the tunnel and it was glorious. The people of the city came out and cheered the runners along. The ministers in Grosse Pointe, one of the suburbs of Detroit, weren't too happy about the race. They felt the runners were upsetting Sunday services. I told the ministers in my column they were missing the point—God's children were running for the glory of life. They didn't like it, but the runners did, and I became an even bigger hero with them.

After the first race, the Motor City Striders—the ones who really put the race together—said they wanted to have a dinner in my honor.

I told them, "Come on, you don't have to do that."

They said, "Oh, yes, we do. We know whose idea this was and we want to thank you." So I got a free dinner and felt very proud.

Not any prouder than Red Smith's review of my book.

He wrote, "Joe Falls' Boston Marathon book should be read twice —first in a single gulp, then one chapter at a time like passages from the Bible."

I should have asked for a raise.

Chapter 12:
Yak, Yak, Yak

Talk shows. Everyone is talking these days, and a lot of people are listening. Or else there wouldn't be talk shows.

They are relatively new, and they're not new at all. One of the best parts of listening to the broadcasts of the Brooklyn Dodgers—aside from the great work of Red Barber—were those three guys who came on after games and jabbered about the Dodgers, baseball, and whatever came into their minds. I loved it. The Yankees didn't do it. The Giants didn't do. But the Dodgers did, and it made, for me, a complete day. It was Bert Lee, Ward Wilson and Bud Greenspan on the occasional show. Greenspan is the man who went on to make all those great films of the Olympics. You sensed these guys weren't stars. They were like the rest of us. Just fans. A little schlocky maybe, but schlock was good. They sounded real, as if they were sitting with us under the street lights at night arguing who was the better short-stop—Phil Rizzuto or Pee Wee Reese. Buddy Kerr—John J. (Buddy) Kerr—played for the Giants but he wasn't good enough to get in on the squabbling. That was OK with the Giant fans because they could shoot Willie Mays at the rest of us when we got around to the centerfielders.

Each night at 7:15, Bert Lee would recreate that day's game, usually the Dodgers, but if the Dodgers didn't play, then one of the other teams. He did it all in 15 minutes, nine whole innings—bang, bang, bang—complete with sound effects. After a while, you could guess when some runs were coming because he'd slow down and set the stage. I wonder if he ever knew he gave this part away.

Red Barber taught me more baseball growing up in New York than anyone else. I was a Yankee fan but listened to the Brooklyn games just because of him. He was a hero...and getting to know him later in life was one of the finest things that ever happened to me.

One spring in Lakeland, the guys went to dinner and a little too much wine was passed around. On the way home in the car, we started recreating The Great Moments in Sports History. I did Lou Gehrig's farewell speech ("I consider myself..."), even Babe Ruth's last appearance at Yankee Stadium when he was dying of throat cancer. I found if I held the microphone to my tape recorder out the window of the car as we were whizzing along, it sounded like the Indianapolis 500. So, I was "Joe Jones in the second turn...here comes A.J. Foyt and he's passing Bobby Unser...now to Jim Smith in the third turn."

When it was George Cantor's turn, he said, "Back goes Gionfriddo. Back, back, back, back, back, back. He...makes a one-hand catch against the bullpen. Oh-ho, Doctor!"

He had it exactly right—Red Barber's call of Gionfriddo's catch against Joe DiMaggio in the 1947 World Series.

I wrote a lot about Barber in *The Sporting News* and he began sending thank you notes. I wrote back, thrilled that he would take the time with me. After several years, I asked if I could visit him at his home in Florida.

I wanted to see him because it sounded as if he was becoming a bit desperate about his career. He was writing everything for everyone, getting into print wherever he could, and I sensed a strange urgency to his work.

We sat in his sun room and I asked why he was doing all this writing.

He looked very sad. He said, "I have no legacy to leave my children or grandchildren. Everything I did on the radio is gone. I hope the printed word will let them know what I did with my life."

I told him of that night in Lakeland, how George Cantor, who wasn't old enough to remember the 1947 World Series, captured his call so perfectly.

"You won't be forgotten," I told him. "You will never be forgotten." I don't know where I got the courage to say such things, but I admired this man so much that I had to tell him what was on my mind.

My radio-TV career started somewhere in the mid-1960s.

This was long before sports became dominant on TV. We got the first television set on our block in 1947. It was one of those seven-inch, black-and-white sets that cost something around $750. The first night we had it was a Saturday and instead of going out with the guys, I sat in the living room with my grandmother (all lights out because that was obviously the best way to watch) and we pulled two chairs as close to the set as possible and watched a movie, "Scattergood Baines," starring Guy Kibbee.

The next year I saw the World Series from Braves Field in Boston and was completely entranced. I can still see Bob Feller's pick-off throw back to second to get Tommy Holmes. The umps called Holmes safe and he came in with the winning run. I think he was out but couldn't be sure. It would be a long time before they developed instant replay.

When the Series shifted to Cleveland, there was no TV. They said the cable didn't stretch that far. It seemed reasonable. I could see this cable running along the ground and getting it from Boston to New York was one thing, but Cleveland to New York was something else.

They started a new TV station in Detroit, Channel 50. They didn't have much dough, so they said they would be an all-sports station. What did it take to send a cameraman and a broadcaster out to a high school game?

Being a man of great vision, I went to station and offered to do a talk show featuring me and George Puscas, whom I worked with at the *Free Press*. They said yes, that quickly, and put us on at 10 o'clock Saturday nights. We would have guests and the viewers could call in and we would kick things around the way they did after the Brooklyn Dodger games.

It worked well for a while. George was a little nervous and his hands would shake. Being a great producer, I asked the cameramen not to show his hands. George was bright and was very well versed in some sports I didn't know much about.

It was a pretty loose operation. We'd start at 10 o'clock and go until there was nothing more to say. It could be 1 a.m. or later. The station didn't care. They had to fill the time some way.

We had Gordie Howe on one night and thought it was great. We talked and talked and talked. One guy called in about midnight and said, "Why don't you guys go to bed so we can watch a movie?"

The highlight was the night Alex Karras was our guest.

He was flying high in those days—the tough-guy, funny-guy character who played for the Detroit Lions. His movie career hadn't started yet but you could sense he was on his way. He was pretty clever.

Puscas was at home at about seven o'clock when he got a call from Karras.

"George, what time is the rehearsal?"

"What rehearsal? We don't have rehearsal. Just show up a little before 10."

"Okay," said Karras. "You want me there at eight o'clock. I'll be on time." He hung up.

We didn't figure it out until later. He was talking from home, talking a little loud, setting up an excuse to get out of the house early. He showed up with a lovely young lady.

I'd brought my 14-year-old son to the studio, and he sat next to Karras' date.

We were going along fine until two boys—17, 18, around there—called up. They asked could they speak to Mr. Karras.

Karras said, "Shoot."

One of the boys said, "Mr. Karras, we have been great admirers of yours for a long time. We think you are a great football player, one of the best in the league. We just wanted to ask you one thing. When was the last time you got (bleeped)?"

I couldn't believe my ears and when we looked at the tape later, I had the dumbest look on my face. I was stunned to silence. George didn't say anything either, but he didn't look dumb.

Karras leaned forward, looked at his date sitting off to the side, and then into the camera and said, "I'm not so concerned about the last time as I am about the next time."

Bang. We were off the air. They went to a commercial and I could feel my face flushing.

"Okay, okay," somebody cried out from somewhere in the room. "We got it. It didn't get on. Relax, everyone."

I didn't know it at the time but they had a seven-second delay and the producer, director or whoever it was stopped the tape before Karras' words got out. When we returned for the next segment, I didn't say a thing. I was still too shaken to speak.

Then it struck me: Did my son hear what he had said? He was sitting right next to the girl. I didn't know how to approach the subject but on the way home in the car, I said: "Mr. Karras is a pretty funny man, eh?"

"Yeah, but what was that he said when he looked at me, I didn't get it."

What luck.

"I don't know...something about the last time he scored a touchdown."

I got my first radio show when Van Patrick's son, working at WQTE, a dawn-to-dusk station in Monroe, a city south of Detroit, committed the cardinal sin of using the "F" word on the air. Somebody had left the door open to his studio and he cried out, "Close the F-ing door!" That was it. Dick Jones, who ran the station, fired him on the spot. The "F" word was one thing the FCC didn't tolerate. Even if it wasn't your fault, they could lift your license. Jones was taking no chances.

He called up and asked how would I like to work for him. I didn't know what to say. I had never thought of going on the radio, not with this New Yawk accent. He said he'd like to have me do two commentaries a day, one in the morning which they'd play three times, and another in the afternoon, which they'd also play three times. He would pay me $12 a show. That was a lot of money, especially when you had five kids.

I worked pretty hard, writing every word and rehearsing very carefully before talking into my tape recorder. Sometimes I had to do it 10 or 15 times before I got it right. Of course the longer I did it, the worse it got. It came out sounding very forced.

I decided on one thing: I would try to involve the listeners. I would do shows that would make them think: Hey, Falls has something this time. Oops, Falls is off the target again. I wanted them to use their minds instead of merely their ears. But I knew I would have to do it honestly or it would have no value. I knew I couldn't fool them. It must have worked because I was on the station for nearly 10 years.

I tried to stay on top of everything, especially in the mornings, after things happened overnight. I'd get up at 5 a.m. and read the papers and listen to the news on the other stations so I wouldn't miss a thing. I was faithful about this except for one morning. I wrote a show without checking into anything. It had something to do with divisional play in baseball. I figured I could get away with it.

That was the morning former heavyweight champion Rocky Marciano died in a plane crash. It was the last time I ever fluffed off my work.

If you are a newspaperman and go on the radio or TV, you cannot serve two masters properly. I thought I could and did everything in my power to do it. But, they are different mediums—competing mediums—and things overlap. You have to make concessions.

When I was hired by WWJ to do commentaries, morning and afternoon again, I asked to talk to all the bosses. I told them I was a newspaperman, first and foremost, and my newspaper would get everything before I put it on the air. They agreed. No arguments. I told them they'd only hired me because I was in the paper and I would do nothing to hurt my paper. Again they said they understood my position. I told them I would come back to them in nine months and make certain we all understood the rules.

"You don't have to do that," they said. "We understand your situation."

I told them: "That's fine. You want me now. But in nine months when I become part of the wallpaper around here, I don't want you coming to me and wondering why I'm putting stuff in the paper before I give it to you."

Very ethical, right? But what happens when a big story breaks at two o'clock in the afternoon and you have a show coming up at 4:15? Do you talk about divisional baseball or do you do what you are trained to do and cover the story to the best of your ability? This happened more times than I liked to think, and it bothered me. I told myself I was a better newspaperman because the radio made me think of more topics than I had ever thought of before. Nice try, Joe. I was only kidding myself.

Today, guys in my business put the cart before the horse and go on the air and blab about everything before putting it in the papers. Amazingly, the papers don't care. In fact, they seem to like it. So what if they're getting warmed up stuff from their writers? Radio and TV make them celebrities, and the papers can cash in on their notoriety.

This is like writing contests. You win a writing contest and the bosses love you. They can extol you, promote you, take credit for you. I have never entered a writing contest in my life. I think they're bunk. If you are a newspaperman, you should be judged by what you do on a daily basis, not a few times a year. Sad to say, this doesn't count as much with your bosses. They love to win contests.

There was—and is, I guess—a restaurant in Salsbury, South Carolina, which decided it would honor sports writers with annual awards. When I was with *The Detroit Free Press*, I won almost every year, something like 10 years in a row. I would never go there to accept their award. While they were well intentioned, I figured they did not know who was good and who wasn't. In time, they got mad at me, thinking I was a big timer who was too good for them. What they never figured out is that I should have won every year. I worked for the only state newspaper in Michigan and got votes from all over the state. How could a guy in Kalamazoo or Bay City compete with me? He couldn't. They finally took my name off the ballot.

The same happened at a national level. I kept finishing second to Jim Murray in the vote. They started asking me why didn't I come to Salsbury to accept my second-place award. I told them the same thing: How could I win when Murray had a syndicate of 200 papers and I only had my paper? I figured the only reason I was even on the ballot was because of my column in *The Sporting News,* which got national distribution. That didn't mean I was better than anyone else; just that I had a better outlet.

Back to talk shows...I was driving home from work one Friday night when one of my colleagues at the paper went on the air and talked for nearly 30 minutes about what was going on at his beat. I thought he did a terrific job, until I picked up the Sunday paper and there was the same stuff he had talked about on the radio. My paper didn't care, and that's the sad part. Whatever became of competition?

I worked for J.P. McCarthy, Detroit's No. 1 radio personality, for three years. I was his morning sports man on WJR three times a week. I got a hundred bucks a show. We worked well together because I respected his expertise as a broadcaster and he respected my knowledge as a sports writer.

One Monday, after the Detroit Lions had lost, he didn't call. I was ready but he never got to me. This was odd because the Lions were always the big story in town, especially when they lost. I didn't say anything, writing it off that this was J.P.'s way. He knew so many people, had so many contacts, that he simply didn't get around to me.

The next week, the Lions lost again. Again he didn't call. Now I knew something was up. When he got off the air at 10 o'clock, I called him and said, "What's going on?"

He said, "What do you mean?"

"I mean the Lions. Two weeks in a row they lose and two weeks in a row you don't call me. Did somebody tell you not to let me talk?"

To his credit, J.P. said, "Yes."

"Who?"

"Russ Thomas."

Thomas was general manager of the Lions. He held the hammer over WJR. The radio station had broadcast rights to the Lions' game and they were not going to put me ahead of those rights. Thomas didn't like me. He didn't like most members of the media. So, he squelched me.

I could understand WJR's position but I could not go on under those conditions. I told J.P., "You are censoring me. I quit."

WWJ hired me almost immediately. I later learned that when people asked J.P. whatever happened to Joe Falls, he told them I wanted more money. I never spoke to him on the air again.

The strange thing is that long after I left—15 years after I left—people kept coming up to me and saying, "We really enjoy you on the J.P. show."

J.P. is gone but that was the hold he had on our community. He was truly tops in his business.

I spent seven years at WWJ and it was a terrific relationship. They let me alone. I could say anything I wanted on the air, "as long as you don't get us into the courts," they said. They were great people to work for, and the pay was excellent: $600 a week. It helped me buy a home. The run ended when they wanted some new voices on the air. I understood. We left on the best of terms.

The mistake with talk radio is they put these people on the air for too long a time. Almost without fail, they know more about sports than I do, but after a while a lot of it becomes repetitive. They can use different words but it comes out the same.

Still, I am amazed at their knowledge. One day a listener called WDFN (The Fan) and asked host Mike Stone, "How are the Denver Broncos doing with their free agent selections?" I said to myself: "Come on, let the guy alone." To my amazement, Stone answered the question.

My fear about talk radio is that I would be exposed as not being up on all sports. What I know, I know pretty well, but I don't know all of it.

Twice I was asked to teach journalism courses in college, by Wayne State University and Oakland University. Not bad for a guy who failed three subjects in his junior year in high school and never went to college.

I told each school: "What a great idea, getting someone in the business to talk to the students, someone who has lived a life as a journalist, working the streets, going behind the scenes, getting to know people, building trusts and confidences...someone who can give them real dope on writing, editing and dealing with people. But I have one problem."

"What's that?" they said.

"What would I say the second day?"

Chapter 13:
Newspapering

Newspaper strikes have not been the bane of my life, but they haven't been much fun, either. I've been in eight of them. And not once did I ever get to vote whether we should be on strike or not. It was always someone else who interrupted my job—the teamsters, mailers, pressmen, etc. As a member of the Newspaper Guild and, later, as a member of management, I never got a chance to say what we should do. Four times my pay stopped, four times it didn't. It didn't matter. I could go out and earn a living. One time I got seven different jobs, each paying $100 a week. I had five kids and had to work.

One strike rubbed out almost all of the 1968 baseball season. It happened when the Tigers were winning the pennant. The strike started the previous November and went on until the following August.

You'd be surprised how many people thought the Tigers were winning because we weren't around to distract them. If we weren't there to bring our readers any bad news, there was no bad news. The players would take care of the good news.

When we started printing in the first week of August, Lee Hills, boss of *The Detroit Free Press,* called a meeting of our sports department. He said we should do our jobs as always but be mindful of how the public felt about us. In other words, don't start any trouble with our stories.

I went on the first trip with the Tigers. It started in Cleveland. Joe Sparma was pitching. He had not given up any hits into the fourth inning but was walking a lot of batters. He led 1-0 but was in constant trouble. Manager Mayo Smith finally pulled him.

I watched Sparma leave the mound. When he got to the dugout, he fired his glove against the back wall. I knew I would have to talk to him after the game.

I approached his locker but he waved me away. He said he had nothing to say. All I could do was write what I saw. The next day, as we were boarding the plane to Boston, Sparma came to me and said, "I want to talk to you when we get on the plane."

I liked Joe. He was a regular guy. Not a good pitcher but a hard worker. He just had too much control trouble. He had been the quarterback at Ohio State but could find his receivers better than he could find home plate.

When I sat down next to him, he started in on his manager. He said Smith had no respect for him; didn't like him, didn't trust him, etc., etc. I knew I had a big story but also remembered what Mr. Hills had told us. I went to Smith for his comments and he said he didn't want to get into a spitting contest with a skunk.

I wrote it and Jack Moss went bonkers.

Jack was sports editor of *The Kalamazoo Gazette,* a longtime friend. This time, he lost it. He wrote a column saying, see, I told you so—the minute the Detroit papers came back there would be trouble. He said Joe Falls started it when he pulled Joe Sparma from the shower after the night game and badgered him until Sparma lit into his manager. Somebody read his column to me over the phone and I could not believe it.

I called Jack. I told him of my concern. He sounded penitent. "I guess it's my fault," he said. "I was mad to see such a negative story right away and I figured this was what happened. Would you like me to write something else and correct it?"

I told him to forget it. The whole thing would blow over and why put him on the spot? Today, we are better friends than ever, which is much better than scoring a minor victory.

The most recent strike at the Detroit papers has been very unsettling. When unions strike, the idea is to shut the plant. That's the leverage. This time, when the unions walked out the front door, the company brought in replacement workers in the back door. *The News* and *Free Press,* now in a Joint Operating Agreement, kept right on printing.

The unions were beaten the first day.

As a member of management I kept my job. I had the title of Sports Editor. I had it because I had it at *The Free Press.* When I switched to *The News,* I asked for the same benefits—hospitalization and insurance. Bill Giles, who was a good boss, said it would be no problem.

It was a problem.

For almost two years, the company couldn't give me the same benefits unless I had a title. Giles asked would I accept the title of Sports Editor. I told him that would be fine, but I was not going to get into the management of the paper—no meetings, suggestions or philosophy. I'd help where I could but I was a reporter and a writer and that's what I wanted to do. Sitting in the office held no appeal for me. I've never had the urge to have power over people. I figured I had enough trouble taking care of myself, much less a whole department of people.

So when the strike started and the writers in the sports department walked out, I stayed. For a short while, I became a one-man writing staff. Some people can write a lot, some can write a little, and some can't write at all. I happen to be one who can write a lot.

Some of the writers who went on strike became upset with me. They felt it was OK if I did my column, but nothing else. They could see our sports page wasn't too bad without them. I wasn't showing off, just doing my job. I've always felt I owed two things to my employer: my loyalty and my best effort. I did not like everything my paper was doing but as long as they were paying my salary, I would give them all I had.

Some of the striking writers—whom I considered close friends —got mad at me. I found this disturbing. All they had to do was talk to me and I would try to explain my position. It was easier for them to get angry. I felt hurt but I did not let it get to me. I figured everyone's feelings were very sensitive and this would pass in time.

After a few weeks, these writers—realizing the strike was working against them—started coming back to work. When they crossed their own picket line, I didn't say anything to them. I just hoped they would learn that I had to do what I had to do, just as they had to do what they had to do.

Now to the Joint Operating Agreement.

This was put into place in 1987, with *The News* and *Free Press* joining forces for what was to be the good of the business. This went against everything I believed in, which was to beat the opposition. *The Free Press* said it would go out of business if it didn't have a Joint Operating Agreement with *The News*. We had beaten them in circulation, both daily and Sunday, and I felt if *The Free Press* couldn't make it, then close up. It was the American way. What I never understood is that *The Free Press* never entertained any offers from prospective buyers. That told me they had a plan that I didn't fully understand.

The original agreement called for *The News* to get 55 percent of the profit for the first five years, then it would be split 50-50 for the next 95 years.

I was wary of the whole thing.

Our circulation at the time of JOA was around 670,000. As I write this, we are down to 220,000. This is one of the largest circulation drops in the history of journalism. We were left largely in the afternoon field, and afternoon papers all over the country were closing up.

I feel journalism in my town has been replaced by bottom-line business, just as it has been with the phone companies, banks, insurance companies and other forms of business. What I never could get is our bosses were in bed with each other but told us we should keep competing against each other. Why, when we shared all the profits?

They had us cold. As journalists, we would naturally compete, and to this day nothing feels better than to beat *The Free Press* on a story, and nothing feels worse than when we are beaten on a story. Just don't think about the partnership.

I got one laugh out of the whole deal. Bob Talbert, a columnist and friend from *The Free Press*—a paper which needed us to survive—wrote on the first day of the JOA: "OK, let's go out now and kick their butts." I wanted to call him and say: "Why didn't you do it before, Robert?" But I didn't.

The best days of my life in the newspaper business were the early days when I worked for The AP in New York and Detroit. Being so young, we were not caught up in the politics. All that mattered was getting good stories, writing them quickly and correctly, and getting them on the wire. They were marvelous times.

I came to Detroit in 1953, arriving from the New York sports department to take over the Sports Editor's job in the Detroit bureau of The AP. I had no idea what I was getting into. Ted Smits, my boss in New York, thought it would be better if I covered everything instead of being No. 17 on his staff.

I arrived at Michigan Central Station at about 7:30 on a Monday morning and no sooner did I walk into The AP office than Charlie Cain, the News Editor, told me I was going to Grand Rapids to cover the Golden Gloves that night. That sounded great, except I had never covered any boxing matches and had no idea where Grand Rapids was or how to get there. He sent me with one of the photographers, and, please, don't laugh at what's coming next: I saw my first lake and my first cow on the ride across the state. We had lakes in Central Park but they didn't seem like lakes, not with all those peanut shells floating in them. These were real lakes, surrounded by trees and grass and blue skies.

I did not know my main job was to provide sports stories for the newspapers around Michigan—some 35 in all, all but one afternoon paper.

We went to The AP office in Grand Rapids, where I met Bud Ashley, who was the correspondent, and was a very mild man. He gave me a warm reception. We were to go to the arena at about six o'clock but he excused himself and said he had to go home for a while. It turned out he went home to give his small children a bath before they went to bed. You can imagine how I felt when Bud, a good friend, died only a few years later.

What was I to do at the fights? I didn't know the fighters, or where they came from, or what they were fighting for. I watched a few bouts, took a few notes, and felt my first big failure in Michigan was about to happen.

Then, a small light went on in my head. A lot of the fighters were getting knocked out, so I excused myself from Bud and went into the dressing rooms. I would ask the fighters what it felt like when they were KO'd.

They were beautiful in their responses, some serious, some humorous. I got a neat story. It was supposed to run only on the state wire because these were all Michigan fighters, but the Detroit bureau offered it for the national sports wire. I was on my way. But not moving all that fast.

I was told to cover the state high school basketball tournament. OK, what's that? It's a tournament involving more than 700 schools in the state. I wondered how I could get around to all these games.

No, dummy, they told me: you sit in the office and take the scores and information over the phone. We'll help you. We'll give you our notes and you write the stories. I would have to do five roundups—Class A, Class B, Class C, Class D and Class E in the Upper Peninsula.

What did all these classes mean, and what was the Upper Peninsula?

The first night wasn't too bad. I watched the other guys take the scores, scribble a few notes, and go on to the next call. I started doing the same. Somebody called in with the score of the Sault Ste.

Marie game in the Upper Peninsula. I typed out the score and out it went on the wire as "Sioux Saint Marie."

My first boxing match took place in Olympia Stadium. It was one of the televised fights on Wednesday night: "What'll you have? Pabst Blue Ribbon. Pabst Blue Ribbon Beer."

The guy who handled the press arrangements was Louie Marudas, a good guy who became a very close friend. We used to eat lamb and okra at his favorite Greektown restaurants. He taught me much about boxing, mostly: "Never judge a fighter until you see him fight hurt."

Louie knew I came from New York and my relatives would be looking in at the fight, so he put me in the front row opposite the camera. I don't say I was a showboat, but I bought a pack of gum and chewed all five pieces during the fight, making sure my family could see me. (Why do I admit such things?)

One of the fighters was Italio Scortichini. I struggled with his name as I was writing my story, trying to beat The UP to the punch. Pretty soon, I started calling him "Scorty," never figuring how that might look in the *New York Times*.

I was anxious to hear from my office when my story was finished. I had done a pretty good job of writing it fast.

The guy on the desk said, "It read OK but what the hell's going on out there?"

"What do you mean?"

"Don't you guys from New York know anything about punctuation?"

"You mean I left out some commas?"

"You left out everything—no commas, no periods, no paragraph marks, no quote marks—no nothing. It came in as one long sentence."

"You're kidding."

"I am not kidding. I will save the copy for you."

I went home feeling terrible. My first fight and it was a complete screw up. The next day I related my tale of woe to Maury Hendry, the Western Union operator who had sent my copy on his machine.

He looked crestfallen.

"It was my fault," he said. "My machine froze up and I couldn't get at any of the punctuations. I couldn't even capitalize the letters. So I just kept sending, knowing your office needed the copy as soon as possible."

I looked at Maury and started laughing, thus starting another long time friendship. The next time we worked a fight, I typed out a page of periods, a page of commas, a page of colons, a page of semi-colons and a few dots and dashes. I gave them to Maury: "Here, sprinkle these throughout my story."

Maury also worked the ball games in Tiger Stadium. All the guys would laugh at him whenever a foul ball came up into the press box. He would go scrambling after it as if his life was on the line.

How many times did I hear, "Go get 'em, Maury"? It was a big joke for a long time...until the day I asked him why did such a thing.

I saw I had embarrassed him.

He said he was getting the balls for Starr Commonwealth, a school for homeless boys in outstate Michigan. I passed this story around quietly, and not only did the guys stop laughing at him, they were flipping him balls that they caught.

The press box at Tiger Stadium has been my home away from home. Tom Gage and his faithful computer figured out that I had spent four years of my life riding in the creaky elevator to and from the press box.

One night I was dictating play-by-play to Tony Adamic, The AP teletype operator. The Tigers were playing the Minnesota Twins and I felt like goofing around. As Harmon Killebrew stepped into the batter's box against Jim Burning, I started giving Tony a fake sing-song call: "Harmon Killebrew became the first player in history to hit a ball over the leftfield roof at Tiger Stadium..."

Tony was laughing.

Moments later, Killebrew connected and sent the ball in a high arc down the leftfield line. It bounced twice on the roof and disappeared from sight. Tony took a look at me, then started wrestling me to the ground. Nobody should be able to make such a call. He rolled me around, his laughter growing louder and louder.

When I saw Killebrew the next day, I told him the story. He said, "I've got one for you."

He said he had five people knock on the door on his hotel room in downtown Detroit and offer him the ball that went over the roof.

Then there was the night I played the role of Chief Peacemaker.

The Tigers had played the White Sox in Chicago and the pitchers were throwing at the batters. Ed Farmer of the White Sox hit Al Cowens of the Tigers and Cowens vowed revenge the next time the White Sox came to Detroit, which was the very next week. The papers played it up big, and more than a few fans turned out expecting fireworks.

If I am against anything in this world, it is violence, exceeded only by cruelty to animals. I didn't like the idea of the game turning into a melee.

I went into the White Sox dressing room. I knew Farmer and he was a good guy. I told him of my concern. I said to him: "What would you do if Al Cowens extended his hand to you?"

He said, "I'd shake it."

Half the job was done. I hustled over to the Detroit dressing room and spoke to Cowens in private. I said the same thing to him: "What would you do if Farmer extended his hand to you?" He said, "I'd shake it."

Farmer and Cowens brought the lineup cards to home plate and shook hands. Both men were smiling. Not many in the crowd realized what was going on. They must have been disappointed when the game was played without incident.

I loved The AP and hoped to work there forever. But I had a tough boss in Detroit—Lou Kramp, who was the Bureau Chief. He was a climber and wanted to reach the top level of management. He thought one way to do it was save the company as much money as possible. He did not like sending his reporters out on assignment. That cost dough. Instead, he ripped stories out of the state papers had our people rewrite them in our office and put them on the wire, as if they were there.

My most important assignment was when they sent me to Ann Arbor for the announcement of the Salk Vaccine. They thought a sports writer could write a colorful side piece. The ballroom on the University of Michigan campus was jammed with reporters. They'd come from all over the world for this momentus occasion—when the dread disease of polio could be wiped out. The officials had the press releases on small carts which they tried to push into the room. When they couldn't get in, they started lobbing them through the air and we scrambled for them.

I'll never forget the first sentence: "It is safe, effective, and potent." Dr. Jonas Salk had done it.

Once again, I choked up on the story. It took me nearly five hours to write 300 words. I went home, exhausted.

The outstate papers liked good coverage on the Tigers. They would assess themselves enough money to send The AP Sports Editor in Detroit to Lakeland each spring. Kramp, on his own, decided the papers did not have to spend this money, even if they wanted to. He cut out the spring training assignment. I was the only AP writer in more than 50 years who did not go to spring training.

The payoff came with the Michigan-Michigan State football game in Ann Arbor.

Kramp said, "If I don't sent you to the game on Saturday, I can save eight bucks in mileage. Come into the office instead and work on the desk."

I couldn't believe this: The AP sports editor in Michigan not allowed to cover the Michigan-Michigan State game? Why was I even in my job? I told him our man in Ann Arbor was not a big sports man—certainly not a football writer—and I probably would have to write the story off the radio.

"Just come into the office," Kramp said.

I came in and, sure enough, the story from Ann Arbor wasn't up to par. Everyone in the office panicked. I started writing the lead from notes I had taken off the radio, putting the Ann Arbor man's name at the top of the story. We got the story out reasonably fast, but not fast enough. The New York sports department questioned us about it. They were never told the truth. Kramp got away with his little trick. I never knew what he did with the eight bucks.

I knew I was finished with The AP. Not because Kramp would not let me go to spring training or because he kept me back from the Michigan-Michigan State game to save eight dollars; it was because he could do these things to the member papers, without their knowledge or consent, and get away it.

I started looking around for another job. I probably should have thought about Ted Smits in New York and how I might disappoint him by leaving The AP. But the truth is I was being pretty selfish. I learned to love Michigan in a very short time and did not want to return to New York.

The Detroit Times, the Hearst afternoon paper, was looking for a baseball writer. Hal Middlesworth of *The Free Press* told me to apply for it.

I told him they wouldn't hire me. Not enough experience.

"Try them," he said.

What I didn't know is that Middlesworth, who once was sports editor of the Oklahoma City Oklahoman, had talked to Edgar Hayes, suggesting I'd be a good hire. I went to Ed and he hired me on the spot.

It was that easy.

The Times was in trouble from the start, feeling a financial pinch that would put it out of business in five more years. But what did I know? I had a good job and was going to work in a place where they had lakes and cows.

The ball games would end around 10:30 and I'd be in the office writing my stories until six o'clock in the morning, with the sun coming up. It was not easy for me, but I enjoyed every minute of my job.

With the paper in deep trouble, the Hearst organization brought in an advertising man named Phil DeBeaubien to run the paper. Right away he thought he was a journalist. He started making all kinds of changes, even shrinking the dimensions of the paper. He made the type larger so it seemed that the readers were getting brighter copy than ever. They were getting less.

DeBeaubien decided he needed a solid pro football writer, so he hired Jack Orr out of New York. I didn't know Orr but I knew his work. It was excellent. He knew how to make a story sparkle. I figured DeBeaubien had finally done something right.

The Lions were opening the season in Baltimore. Orr was to go from New York to Baltimore and cover the game, then fly to Detroit to begin his new job.

The game was played on the last Sunday of the baseball season. I wasn't sent to Cleveland because the games didn't mean anything. It was a way to save a little money.

I listened to the game on the radio, then went to the office to wrap up the baseball season. Jack Saylor, our night desk man, looked worried.

"What's the matter?" I asked.

"I haven't heard from our new football writer yet and the Lions' game has been over for three hours."

Jack waited another hour, then came over to my desk. Still no Orr. Saylor said, "You see the football game on TV today?"

"Yeah, sure. Why?"

"Do you think you can do a story? I've got some statistics and quotes off the wire. You can work those in."

I wrote the story and put Jack Orr's name on it. Sure enough, here was Phil DeBeaubien marching into the sports department the next day, slapping the paper with his hand and saying: "Now this is the kind of stuff we need in this paper. This is what you call good writing."

I tried to slink under the desk but couldn't quite make it.

DeBeaubien went around town that week brandishing the paper and bragging about his new hire. On Thursday, somebody told him what had happened. He came into the sports department, glared at me, and left.

I should have been given a chance to write the column. I wasn't quite ready but I was more ready than anyone else in the department. DeBeaubien was so mad he went out and hired Ron Smith, the golf writer at *The Free Press*. He did it because of one line Smith had written about little Jerry Barber, the golfer. He said, "Barber is no bigger than the tiny 9s on the gasoline station signs."

"That," said DeBeaubien, "is what I called good writing."

I suppose I should have been mad at Ron, but I wasn't. It wasn't his fault what happened. We became friends and went on a lot of assignments together and had some good times.

The Free Press, miffed at losing its golf writer, tried to hire me. I went to Edgar Hayes with their offer. He said, "What will it take you to stay?" I told him 25 bucks a week. He said, "You've got it." I never got it, and a few months later the paper went out of business.

Chapter 14:
Mantle and Maz

The World Series. I saw Don Larsen's perfect game, Bill Mazeroski's home run, Kirk Gibson's two home runs and even felt the ground shake in San Francisco. I'd like to tell you about Max Lapides.

Max is a friend of mine, a long-time Detroiter. He has loved the Tigers for all his life, and when they got down to the seventh game against the Cardinals in 1968, he had to go to St. Louis. He simply had to be there.

He took a morning flight, saw the Tigers win, and took the first flight back to Detroit. They had beaten Bob Gibson and Max could have flown home without an airplane. He was that ecstatic.

One problem. The plane never landed in Detroit. The fans were so excited about winning the World Series, they overran the airport. All incoming flights had to be detoured to other cities. Max wound up in Dayton. Dayton-Schmaton. So what? The Tigers were champions of the world and when the passengers, mostly Detroiters, got off the plane, they went to the bar and started partying.

They were singing and dancing and drinking. Max noticed one guy sitting in a corner by himself. He didn't seem to be having much fun.

He went over to him and said, "What's the matter, Buddy? Something wrong? Don't you know the Tigers are champions of the world?"

"You're telling me," the guy said.

"Come on, cheer up. We'll get home yet."

"My home is in Oklahoma City," he said. "My plane stopped in St. Louis and all you crazies got on. I'm supposed to be married in

Detroit today. My fiancee is waiting for me in the Detroit airport and I don't know when I'll ever see her."

The World Series.

I saw my first one in 1942. It was the Yankees against the St. Louis Cardinals in Yankee Stadium. We got up at 6 a.m. and got to the stadium at 8 a.m. We wanted to be sure to get in. Our hearts sank when we saw the line. It went around the stadium and two blocks more, eight or 10 deep. We would never make it.

When the gates opened at 8 a.m., the line moved swiftly—so fast we had to run to keep up. I couldn't believe it. We sat in right-centerfield because that was the closest spot, and I had my faithful dice with me.

I'd dreamed up a game of baseball that you could play with dice. You'd read the lowest number first: 2-6 or 3-4. It took a long time to perfect the right system. Too many of the scores were too high but you could play a 3-2 game once in a while, and the fun was in the announcing.

I was with my cousin and a friend and I brought my scorebook and we took turns playing against each other. I got so excited at one point that I dumped a whole cup of Coke over the man sitting in front of us. I was appalled. I kept trying to dry him off with my hankie while apologizing all over the place. He was soaked but was pretty good about it.

Two hours later we were still playing our dice games and I got carried away again and dumped another cup of Coke over him. I can't remember what was said this time but I never threw the dice again that day. The Yankees lost with Terry Moore of the Cardinals going into right-center to rob Joe D. of a triple, but who cared? I felt like hiding in a hole.

I covered my first World Series as a baseball writer in 1956. That's when Larsen pitched his perfect game against the Dodgers in Yankees Stadium. It was also the first time I'd ever ridden in a limo. We were staying at the Commodore Hotel on 42nd Street and Lexington Ave., and I was up on the mezzanine balcony waiting for a cab. John Fetzer, owner of the Tigers, came along and asked if I'd like to ride in his limo to the stadium. The only other time I've been in a limo (what a sheltered life) was at a Muhammad Ali fight in Houston. Trainer Angelo Dundee saw me sitting alone in the lobby of the hotel and said, "Come on, we're going to dinner. You're coming along with us." Good man, Angelo.

I was working for *The Detroit Times*, an afternoon paper, and as Larsen's run of hitless innings grew longer and longer, I got a call from Ed Hayes, my boss. He said they could make some late-afternoon editions if he pitched a no-hitter or a perfect game and he needed a story when the game ended.

I could not do it that quickly. It was the seventh inning and I decided to take the tack that Larsen would pitch a perfect game and started banging away on my typewriter. I never saw a thing in the seventh, eighth or ninth innings, not even Dale Mitchell's strikeout for the final out. I kept my head down, trying to find the right words. When something happened I'd say to the guys next to me: "What happened?" They'd tell me, I'd scribble it in my book and go on typing. So when I say I saw Larsen's perfect game, I really didn't see it.

The next big one was Bill Mazeroski's home run against the Yankees in 1960. That's the one which clinched the World Series for the Pittsburgh Pirates, and I can still see Yogi Berra going back for the ball against the leftfield wall in Forbes Field and watching him look up as it sailed out of sight.

It was a difficult moment for me. I was old enough to know better, but I was still a Yankee fan. I felt suffocated. But I knew I had to do my work. My feelings for the Yankees had fallen away when I became a baseball writer and saw them up close. They were very arrogant, even nasty. Mickey Mantle, Whitey Ford, Billy Martin and Clete Boyer always seemed to be laughing at those around them, mostly the newspapermen, making them look stupid whenever they could. These players had been my heroes; now they were very distasteful people.

Mantle was a little different than the others. When he was around Martin, Ford and Boyer, he could be a smart aleck, very cutting, trying to get laughs from them. When you got him alone, he was much different. He was pleasant and cooperative, and this is the Mickey Mantle I chose to remember when he died.

Anyway, when I walked into the Yankee dressing room that day, Mantle was sitting in front of his locker with his head down. He was crying, and the tears were spotting the floor. I knew, in that moment, the measure of the man. He was a big star—a celebrated figure—but he was also an athlete, and now he was crushed.

At that moment, Elroy Face, Pittsburgh's great relief pitcher, appeared in the doorway. I thought he had come over to offer his congratulations or condolences to the Yankees.

He had an awful expression on his face. He looked around the room and said, "F you guys!"

Some memory.

The next year, in Cincinnati, the Yankees were mauling the Reds. Mantle was out of the lineup. They said he had a hole in his back the size of a silver dollar. I didn't know what that meant. How do you get a hole in your back the size of a silver dollar? They said he was hurting a lot.

Midway through the game, here came Mantle out of the dugout to pinch hit. How bad could he be, I thought. When he stepped into the batter's box, I could see a black spot on the back of his shirt that was growing larger and larger. It was blood, running out of the hole in his back. My estimate of the man went up, way up.

I saw the Mets beat the Orioles in 1969 and the fans tore up the field. They gouged out the grass, wrote on the outfield walls and carried on. Some said it was the greatest celebration in history.

It wasn't even close.

Pittsburgh in 1960 was the wildest I had ever seen. After leaving the Yankee dressing room, I walked back to my hotel, which wasn't too far away. Already the streets were filled with debris—newspapers, magazines, ticker tape...the sort of stuff you see in newsreels. By the time I got to the hotel, the newspapers were up to my knees. Music filled the air as record shop owners put their phonographs out on the street and turned up the sound. Everyone was dancing.

I could not get into my hotel until I showed them identification and my key. The noise in my room was deafening. I felt like I was sitting in the middle of 10 Indianapolis 500s. My room wasn't air-conditioned, so I had a choice. I could leave the window open and get whatever air was available or I could close it and take the chance of suffocation. I went for the suffocation.

Detroit in 1968 was even bigger. It was a city-wide celebration, not just downtown. My son took my car and drove it to the airport to welcome home the Tigers from St. Louis. He took his friends along. They blew the horn so much they killed the battery and had to leave the car near a field. I had to go back and get it the next day.

And then we have 1984, when my city went wild after the victory over San Diego. We burned police cars, turned over other cars, set fires, got into fights, engaged in muggings and even killed one man at a downtown hot dog spot. Shameful. After the 1967 riot, the largest in history in which 43 people died and millions of dollars in property damage was reported, Detroit was viewed as the most dangerous city in the land. I'm not sure if we've ever lived down that reputation. After the Detroit Pistons won the first of their two NBA titles in 1988, nine people were killed in the streets that night. Nine.

The World Series used to be such a pleasant experience. I even caught a foul ball in the 1959 classic in the Los Angeles Coliseum. They had 93,000 in the place that day. When Nellie Fox of the White Sox fouled one back into the auxiliary press box, it bounced off the hands of several guys and landed in my lap as I was typing. I call it my 93,000-to-1 shot, and wish I could do as well in the lottery.

When I was young, the World Series was played during the day, which meant we were in school. Sometimes the teachers would let us listen on the radio, but sometimes they wouldn't. We had to come up with a plan. We would take turns raising our hands and asking to go to the bathroom. We'd space these out every 15 minutes. We kept a radio in the bathroom and each guy would get the score. When we got back to our room, we would hold our fingers against our chest to signify the number of runs scored. The left hand was the visiting team, the right hand the home team.

Today, the World Series isn't nearly as much fun. The games start late and finish late. Some of them seem to drag on forever. Many kids have to be in bed. I can't understand why they don't play a couple of day games. But, this is the era of marketing and money, marketing and money, and they will only do what will produce the most money. (What do they do with all that money, anyway?)

So many writers cover the World Series that it has become a mob scene. If you are in the main press box, fine. But if you have to sit in the auxiliary press box, then it's not so fine. You are a great distance from the game, and everything seems like a rumor. You can stay in the working room and watch TV. Many do. I've done it many times. But I'm not so sure if my office sends me on the road to watch TV. I do it because my job is to write stories, and do it as quickly as possible, and TV is the only way to go.

I think all this is called progress.

Chapter 15:
Fore on the Floor

There are three things I've never done in my life. I've never shot a birdie, caught a trout or kissed a redhead. My wife says I can kiss all the trout I want.

Actually, I shot one birdie. It was the first year I played golf, around 1948. I went to the Bayside (N.Y.) course and played by myself. It took six hours or so to get around, and when the bus stopped to take me home, I was so tired I couldn't climb up the steps. I sat on the curb for an hour or so before I got my strength back. In my neighborhood, the bus stop was at the bottom of a steep hill. The bus bounced when it came to a stop, shuddering something awful. My buddies would stand there and when the bus would shake to a stop, they'd put their foot up on the steps, tie their shoelaces, thank the driver and walk away. I cannot repeat what some of the drivers said to them.

Anyway, I got a birdie that day, a two on a par three. I got no more in the next 40 years. Not a one. Believe it. I played eight or nine times a season, mostly at charity events. I was a 110-125 shooter and never came close again.

Yet, I like this game. I like to watch it, talk about it, read about it and write about it. I just don't like playing it. I've seen four British Opens, countless U.S. Opens and Masters, and many PGAs. I like the sport because the players are so cooperative—the best of all to interview. Auto drivers are next. All you have to do is catch them when they're not working on the cars.

I asked Jack Nicklaus why golfers were such good interviews. He said, "It's because of you guys in the press. You were always there to meet us at the final hole to ask us questions, and we got used to it."

I choose not to argue with this man but I think he is wrong. I believe golfers are so easy to get along with because many of them went to college and grew up in a country club environment, where bad conduct was not tolerated. Then, too, the golfers behave themselves better than any other athletes. They cannot drink, take drugs or stay out too late too often or else it will affect their performance, and this is one sport where they have to make it on their own and cannot afford to be at less than their best.

One golfer who didn't go to school was Sammy Snead.

When he was getting near the end of his playing days, he came into the press hut at Augusta for an interview. He was asked how much longer he could go on.

"I'm thinking of retiring," said Snead. We all sat up. This was a story.

"Yep," he went on, "I'm thinking of turning in my clubs and getting me a nice job in Washington, D.C. I figure I'll become a political cartoonist."

We looked at him, not believing what we were hearing.

"It would be a good job," Snead said. "I'd go into the office and all I'd have to do was have one idea a day. But I've been a-thinking about it. I think I'll become a sports writer . . . because then I won't have to have any ideas."

When I was given my first column at *The Free Press* in 1965, I wasn't sure how to go about it. I did the first few reasonably well, then I ran out of ideas. Some guy in the office said that Walter Hagen, the old pro, lived in Traverse City in Northern Michigan and why didn't I go up there and do a piece on him.

I didn't know Hagen, except that he was a great name in golf. I went to the phone, got his number from information and dialed it.

The phone rang several times before someone picked it up. I didn't hear anything on the other end of the line.

"Hello."

I waited. No response.

"Hello. Is anyone there?"

I thought I could hear someone breathing but I couldn't be sure.

"Hello. This is Joe Falls of *The Detroit Free Press.* Is anyone home?"

Finally, a woman's voice came on the line. She identified herself as Doris Brands, Walter Hagen's housekeeper, and apologized for the delay. She said Mr. Hagen had picked up the phone but was unable to speak because of his throat cancer and was there anything she could do for me?

I didn't know what to say, but mumbled something about coming to see Mr. Hagen to write about him. I didn't know about the cancer.

She said, "That would be lovely. When can I tell Mr. Hagen you will be here?"

"How about tomorrow?"

"Tomorrow would be fine," she said. She gave me directions and I put the phone down, my hands trembling.

I drove to Traverse City and found their cabin in the woods, overlooking Long Lake. The housekeeper met me at the door and was as pleasant and polite as the day before. She led me into a large room overlooking the lake, where Hagen was standing and grinning at me. He was smoking a cigarette and had a white bib around his neck.

We shook hands but I didn't know what to say.

The housekeeper said, "Mr. Hagen is glad to see you. I can do talking for him. We both understand sign language."

It may have been the most marvelous two hours of my life. We chatted like mad, me talking, Hagen making his signs and gestures, and the housekeeper translating. In no time at all, I felt at ease.

Finally, I knew it was time to go and got up to leave. Hagen made some sounds toward the housekeeper, who said, "Mr. Hagen would like to know if you'd like to see him hit a golf ball?"

"Love to!"

He went to the corner of the room and pulled a club from a golf bag leaning against the wall.

He came back to the middle of the room and placed an imaginary ball on the carpet. I watched, transfixed.

He took his stance, drew his club back and swung through the invisible ball. He looked out the large picture window and let out a loud whoop, making more noises to his housekeeper.

"Oh," she said. "Mr. Hagen made a perfect shot—right into the middle of the lake!"

My favorite golfer has been Jack Nicklaus, partly because he has been so good but partly because he is such a great emissary for his game. Arnold Palmer had a natural way with people. Nicklaus had to learn it. At the start, he could not suffer fools. He had to learn how to conduct himself, which is always hard to do, but he did it, and I have had nothing but admiration for him.

We were talking once in Florida. I'd gone there for the Breeder's Cup and had to do a magazine piece on Nicklaus. As always, he was cooperative. I asked one question I always wanted to ask, "What does it feel like to have so much money? I mean, you get $35,000 to have lunch and play some customer golf. What does that feel like?"

I told him this interested me because the most money I ever had at one time was $6,000, an advance I got for writing a book on the Boston Marathon.

"That's it? Six thousand dollars?" he asked.

"That's it," I told him.

"I'll be darned."

This was on a Friday. The phone in my hotel room rang Sunday morning. It was Nicklaus. He said, "I told my wife what you said about the $6,000. She didn't believe me. Here, I'll put her on the phone and you tell her."

"That's right, Barbara. Six thousand bucks."

She said, "I'll be darned."

Chi Chi Rodriguez has been a longtime favorite. How can you not like this man—this man who cares so much for others, especially the children? When he came to my town for the 1996 Ford Seniors Open, I asked him to play the name game: I'd give him a name and he'd give me the first thing that popped into his head.

He was very good. Madonna: "Could have been a great singer but if she put on a show, I would be a no show." He topped himself when I mentioned the Pope. He said, "He tells women not to take the pill. If you don't play the game, don't make the rules."

My problem with golf is the days are too long. I'm a nap guy. I usually need a nap a day to keep going, but where can you lay down at a golf tournament? I'd set up sleeping rooms for us old geezers—a dark room, with clean cots, for a little shut eye.

St. Andrews was my first British Open and I got tired one day and went behind the press tent to take a nap. I laid down next to a dumpster. Somebody took my picture and posted it in the press room. It hangs in my den.

I went off into the bushes at Royal Lythem & St. Annes looking for 40 winks. A British Bobby woke me with a poke of an umbrella. Some fans had told him there was a dead man in the gorse.

My friends at the Buick Open in Flint took very good care of me. I was slumbering under a tree when they got beer bottles and placed them all around my inert body. This time I was awakened by the laughter of the fans.

Chapter 16:
Big Red and Maverick

It was a rainy Saturday morning in Lexington, Kentucky. We were covering the NCAA basketball tournament. The writers were having breakfast in the coffee shop when I stood up and said, "Anyone want to see Secretariat today?" Hands shot up all around the room.

A mistake. I could only take five in my car. It seemed like two dozen wanted to go. I said, "You guys settle it, I'll meet you in the lobby in 10 minutes."

I had made arrangements with the people at Claiborne Farm in nearby Paris, Kentucky, to have an audience with the great horse. You always had to call ahead. But they always said yes, and were very kind and courteous in every visit. They knew what they had—maybe the greatest race horse of all time—and were willing to share him with others.

I'd been to see Big Red any number of times and knew exactly where he was. He was in the first field off to the right, behind that row of bushes. You could not see him right away, but you could hear him. He knew when somebody was coming and he'd race over to the fence and stand there and wait for you.

That's what happened on this morning. Big Red was a ham. He loved to see people. He even knew when they were going to take his picture. He would stand straight and those ears would go up.

We could hear the rustle behind the bushes as we approached his spot. We knew he was there, and he knew we were coming. And there he stood, a regal figure on this misty morning, looking at us with those large round eyes.

I stepped forward and said, "Good morning!"

One of the guys behind me said, "No, no, no."

I turned around.

He stepped forward.

He said, "Good morning, SIR!"

I loved this horse. I loved him for a lot of reasons. I knew little about horse racing. It took me a long time to figure out what a furlong was, but it didn't matter. The beauty of these animals was overpowering. It was Billy Reed, the great Kentucky writer, who put it best when he said we all seek perfection in life, and no where do we get closer to it then when we are around these three-year-old thoroughbreds, at the peak of their lives, so sleek, so strong, so powerful.

Besides, I was courting my second wife at the time of the Triple Crown races in 1973 and took her to the races. We were there when Secretariat set the track record in the Kentucky Derby and again when he swept to victory in the Preakness.

Now it was the Belmont Stakes in New York. No horse had won the Triple Crown in a quarter of a century and the track was packed to see if this running machine could do it. Mary Jane couldn't make it because she had to work. But I did and it was the most memorable experience of these 50 years.

The press box was jammed. Writers came in from all over the country—writers who never paid attention to the sport of kings. They sensed history in the making and wanted to be part of it.

Secretariat won by 31 lengths, and nobody wins by 31 lengths. I will never forget what happened in the press box when he went under the wire. Nothing happened. Nobody spoke. Nobody moved. We were stunned into disbelief.

I was standing between the chart callers for The Racing Form. One of them was a friend. He had a strange expression on his face. He said to his colleague: "I have 31 lengths." His colleague said, "I have 31 lengths." My friend said, "We'd better wait for the film."

None of us could believe what we had seen. It was the single greatest performance I had ever witnessed.

I went back to see Big Red many times, touching him, petting him and thanking him for making my courtship days so happy. And then the word came when I was with the Tigers in Chicago: they had to put Big Red down because of a foot infection. I sat in my room and wept. A grown man crying over a horse. I did not go to the ball game that night.

I've visited his grave several times. They buried his entire body. Usually, it is only the head, the hooves and the heart. This time they did it all, and each time I have visited Clairborne Farm, I have wept. Please try to understand; I can't fully explain this, either.

As I said earlier, a guy once asked, "Do you like games or events?" Smart guy. I knew what he meant. Was I a baseball-football-basketball-hockey man or did I prefer tennis, golf, horse racing, sailing, the Olympics: the events?

I told him: "I prefer the events."

One reason is that the venues were always changing, and I loved to see new things. After 5,000 baseball games, 5,001 isn't very stimulating. But how about going to Moscow for the Goodwill Games?

I did that in the late 1980s. It was scary, but memorable. They put me in a hotel across from the Kremlin and what was so interesting is that I couldn't lock my door. It didn't have a lock. Here I am in the heart of Russia, our old enemy, and I can't lock my door. That might have been okay but they had a KGB officer on every floor. I used to smile at them and say hello when I got off the elevator. But they sat there behind their desk and looked at me with a stone-like expression on their face. What I did was pile as much furniture as possible against the door, especially the table lamp. If somebody tried to get in during the night, I would hear the crash of the lamp. Nobody tried to get it. Who's paranoid? I was paranoid.

They told us at the U.S. press center that our rooms were bugged, so don't talk on the phone, don't talk in the room, just be quiet. I was sending back a radio show one day, saying how the stores and shops were so empty and people shuffled through the streets carrying bags, satchels and valises, in case something became available. Whenever this happened, lines would quickly form and people would wait a long time to make a purchase. I was in the middle of the show when the phone connection went out, and I could not get another one from my room. Were they listening in? What do you think?

Two things impressed me.

The taxi cab drivers were not paid by the number of fares they took, but by the hour. If they didn't want to pick you up, they didn't pick you up. I had dozens and dozens of cabs pass me by, and I wondered how they knew I was an American.

Secondly, the street lights were very dim. They cast a dull orange glow which put a depressing feeling over the entire city. I was supposed to stay for seven days but I'd had enough after six. I often wonder what all these Russian hockey players think now that they can live in America. Viacheslav Fetisov's wife had a terrific comment when asked about life in the United States. She said, "I cannot believe it—six kinds of mayonnaise."

One light moment about Moscow, though.

The first morning, I tried to order breakfast in the hotel restaurant but the waiters could not understand me. I went in search of someone who could speak a little English. I was walking down a hallway when I met two women in white uniforms. I pointed to my mouth and said, "Eat. Eat. Eat."

They looked at each other and smiled. They took me by my arms and led me around the corner into a dentist's office.

Since I had been a baseball-football-basketball-hockey man all my life, I was excited about seeing my first Indianapolis 500. All the guys said wait'll I see the start of the race. I won't believe it. They said it was the most exciting moment in sports.

I'd heard this for weeks, and now I was hearing it again in the press box. I was working with Bob Latshaw of *The Free Press.* He liked to get to the track early, like 7 a.m. The race didn't start until 11 a.m. but he liked to be ready.

So I sat there for four hours hearing more words of wonder about this race. I had never heard a car warm up and now I was going to see 33 of them at once, tearing down that main straightaway.

And, finally, here they came—faster, harder and louder than I ever imagined. I backed away from my spot in the front row and half turned from the track. I was frightened.

And then it happened.

This was the 1966 race where the whole thing blew up before they ever got to the first turn. The cars started twisting and turning, slamming into each other, ramming into the walls, with smoke and tires flying all over the place.

I thought they were all dead and in my inimitable fashion, I cried out, "Stop the race! Stop the race!"

Seventeen cars went out but the only injury was to A.J. Foyt. He got a splinter in the back of his thumb as he was climbing the fence to safety.

I was so shaken I got a headache that seemed to split my head apart. I did not pay much attention the rest of the way. When it was over, with head still throbbing, I started my column saying, "Stop this senseless slaughter."

When I was almost done, I turned and saw my son sitting down a ways in the press box. He was holding something in his lap. It was a nose cone off one of the cars. I had taken him, a neighbor and his son to the race, and now I turned to my neighbor and said, "Tell him to get rid of that thing! I don't want to see it when I'm done."

My neighbor told me to take it easy. He said, "It's a trophy. He is proud of it. Let's talk about it later."

After the crash, my son had gone onto the the track and retrieved the nose cone. I cooled down a bit and let him keep it. As we were walking though Gasoline Alley to get to our car, I walked behind my son. I didn't want anyone to think I had anything to do with that nose cone.

People stopped him. They asked about what he had. Some started taking his picture. I looked on in wonder. I put my arm around my son. Why not be in the pictures? Shame on me.

It took almost six hours to drive home, and for six hours all we did was talk about the race, especially the massive pileup. I couldn't ever remember talking baseball or football for six straight hours, so the next day I thought I would try something. I took the nose cone to my office and placed it on the slot desk in the sports department.

I said nothing to no one. The nose cone was painted red, yellow and black and a tire mark ran over the top of it. Word got around and before the day was over, I don't know how many people in the building came to see this oddity. All it was was a piece of fiberglass but they studied it, touched it, and talked about it with great interest.

Maybe there was more to auto racing than I realized. I found out this was the nose cone off the car of Billy Foster, and it turned out it was his car which started the chain reaction smash up.

The man who built the car was Jim Robbins, an industrialist in suburban Troy, so I went out to talk to him.

"They were going too fast," I said.

He said, "No, they were going too slow. My man ran over the wheel of a slower car in front of him and that set the whole thing off."

I must have written seven straight columns on auto racing, and I still didn't know much about the sport. The next year, Foster was killed in an accident in Milwaukee and Jim Robbins perished when his jet plane blew up on takeoff.

I was drawn back to the track but always with a feeling of guilt. Was I there for the accidents or the competition? I could not understand how those drivers could even get into their cars when the penalty could be so severe.

I asked Mario Andretti about this and he said, "Suppose you're driving to work one day and you see the worst accident you've ever seen out on the highway. You drive by slowly and look at it, and then you find out it involved your best friend. What do you do? Do you stop driving to work? No. You have to make a living. That's what we do. This is how we make our living. So we go on."

I hung on these words for a long time but my guilt increased as the drivers were dying before my eyes or getting severely injured. I tried to rationalize my feelings but all this led to were a lot of poorly-written columns. I was in about a four-year slump at Indy and nearly quit going there altogether. I felt I was helping to perpetuate a blood sport.

Finally, it dawned on me. I could moralize all I wanted, but they didn't need me there to run. They would run anyway, no matter how I felt. I realized my job was not to sit in judgment of them but to be the best sports writer I could be, and ever since then, I have been able to handle this sport with a clear mind.

Besides, you get to meet people like James Garner.

I am slightly ga-ga about movie actors; I swoon over them the way fans do with athletes. One day, there was Garner standing by the tower looking out over the parking lot. I caught my breath.

When I first started writing from Indy, Garner was in the film "Grand Prix," the story of the Formula I circuit in Europe. He was Pete Aaron, the American, who drove for a Japanese company and won the driving championship. I loved that film. I saw it, by actual count, 16 times.

Now I carefully approached Garner. I knew this man was Maverick, one slick dude. I knew I could not walk up to him and say, "Hello, Mr. Garner. I'm Joe Falls of The Detroit Free Press. May I talk to you for a moment?"

I sidled up to him as he was searching through the parking lot. I pretended to be searching through the parking lot.

I said, "Grand Prix, 16 times."

I knew this would get him.

But he didn't look at me. He simply said, "Not a record."

Post Game Notes

Where do we go with sports in the next century? As long as there is television—and it can only get better and better, until we see images in three dimension on the walls of our home (you can reach out and all but touch the athletes)—sports will flourish. And more money than ever will be turned over by our games. I just don't know if I could afford $45 hot dogs.

I do not get excited about world wide competition (Chicago at Leningrad, Seattle at Hong Kong) because more athletes and more teams only will muddle the sports scene. I have enough trouble figuring who is the coach of the Phoenix Coyotes or who is playing quarterback for the New Orleans Saints to take on a whole new set of names and faces—names and faces we will know little about—and see only on occasion.

But, as we reached out for the moon, we will reach out for more sports around the globe because it is the natural thing to do. It will seem exciting and hold our interest for a while. But by 2050, I see the whole thing settling down. We will become more comfortable with our own teams, playing in our own areas, and not concern ourselves with what goes on in Peking, Buenos Aires and New Delhi. Worldwide sports will be fun for a while, just as it was fun when they first started showing us events from Europe. Who wouldn't want to see a ground rule double bounce over The Great Wall of China? But, in time, the novelty will wear off. It will all be accepted and our interest will level off.

If I am wrong about this, you can write me at...well, I'm not exactly sure what my next address will be. And if you don't like this book, I will try to live another 50 years and write another one.

I am sure of one thing, though: We will always have our games, even if the form changes. That's because we are a competitive people, and a society that seeks enjoyment out of sports. We love to live vicariously, even if we can't throw up a jump shot or snare a rebound and put it past the goalie.

I don't think baseball will die, as some predict, and even hope. Football will remain strong and become the dominant sport because it appeals to our basic instincts. I fear the interest in hockey and basketball may fade because of too many teams in too many places. They may overexpose themselves to the point that we adopt a so-what attitude when the big games roll around. I fear the seasons may become too long, until they virtually play the year round.

Mostly, I see sports on TV dominating the lives of many people —even as they are asked to pay for this entertainment in their own homes. I have never paid a dime to watch any of the closed-circuit fights on TV, but when this becomes the only way that sports is available to the public, I believe the public will summon up the bucks to see these games. In fact, this will become part of the family budget, along with food, clothing, transportation and the other necessities of life. We will not give up our enjoyment.

As my business—newspapering—becomes less and less effective, television will take almost complete command of our lives. That's why this industry has the greatest responsibility of all as we turn into the next 100 years.

They may entertain us—thrill us with their magnificent pictures—but they should maintain their integrity in presenting their programs to us. No shilling, no schlock, for the benefit of the bucks. Maybe I ask too much because when money is the issue, many of our values are put aside. I see TV recognizing its responsibility but not until the middle of the century, when, after realizing it has the entertainment market to itself and cannot produce any more revenue, the industry will start looking to other areas of expertise and begin doing a more credible job than ever. The government, which will somehow get in on the cash flow, will insist on it.

Personally, I hope the leftfield wall in Fenway Park stands for another hundred years, and the vines flourish forever on the outfield walls of Wrigley Field. Again, this is too much to ask but an old man is allowed to dream because these were the days he knew best and he wouldn't trade them for anything.

There will never be another man like my man, Theodore Samuel Williams.

You get only one in a lifetime. The Kid will live forever in this mind.

By the way, does anyone happen to have Kim Novak's phone number?

Bill Walsh: Finding the Winning Edge
$24.95

A business-style book that illustrates and outlines the basic organizational, coaching, and system philosophies that Bill Walsh used throughout his career with the San Francisco 49ers. The coach of the decade for the 80s reveals how after being out of professional coaching for 9 years, he still has more influence on the NFL than any current coach.

Richard Petty: The Cars of the King
$34.95

This is a must read for the diehard race fan or modeler. Study the career of Richard and automatically trace NASCAR's growth. With Richard's pioneering, see how the sport developed from the racing of showroom stock cars to the specialized stock cars in racing today.

Richard Petty: The Cars of the King

(leatherbound edition) Autographed by Richard Petty. Limited edition of 500 copies. Only $99.95! Available from Sports Publishing, Inc. only, call 1.800.327.5557.

John Fetzer: On a Handshake $22.95

Author Dan Ewald tells the story of how the Tiger owner's shaping of the 1968 and 1984 World Series champions and his pioneering decisions that helped shape the game. The book explains how Fetzer embraced a romantic appreciation for the game and how baseball symbolized America's national essence.

John Fetzer: On a Handshake

(2 leatherbound editions)
* Autographed by Hall of Famer George Kell. Limited edition of 300 copies. $39.95.
* Autographed by five 1968 Tigers, Mickey Lolich, Bill Freehan, Willie Horton, Jim Northrup, and Gates Brown. Limited edition of 300 copies. $49.95.

Both limited edition Fetzer books are available from Sports Publishing, Inc. only, call 1.800.327.5557.

All titles are available at your local bookstore or by calling 1.800.327.5557